TRUTH OF THE HEART
an anthology of George Fox
1624-1691

collated, edited and annotated by

Rex Ambler

with a translation into modern English

revised edition 2007

QUAKERbooks

First published in September 2001.

This second edition with minor revisions published April 2007.

Quaker Books, Friends House, 173 Euston Road, London NW1 2BJ

www.quaker.org.uk

We acknowledge with thanks the use, on our front cover, of
The Quakers Meeting – engraved by J. Bowles from a painting by
Egbert van Heemskerk (1645-1704) – from the Library of
Friends House, London.

© Britain Yearly Meeting and Rex Ambler 2001 and 2007

ISBN 978 0 901689 65 8

Copy editor: Seren Wildwood

Design & typesetting: Jonathan Sargent

Text typefaces: Stempel Garamond & Joanna

CONTENTS

PREFACE TO THE REVISED EDITION

The call for a reprint of this book has given me the opportunity to make a few changes in the text. There were some errors of printing in the first edition that went unnoticed; these have been corrected. And I have changed my mind on how best to translate some of the extracts into modern English. In extracts 1:27, 84, 125, 129; 2:93; 3:31, 71 I have found a neater way of conveying Fox's sense. In 1:16; 3:84 I have come to understand Fox's meaning differently – in one line in both cases. I have also added to some endnotes for clarification. These are all minor changes. They have made me aware, however, that translation is always a risky enterprise, and though much can be gained by it, something may be lost as well. So it is important that the old and new versions stand side by side. I would encourage readers to look at the translation always in comparison with the original text.

A few people have raised the question whether it is advisable, or even possible, to render Fox into modern English. Would we do the same with Shakespeare? My first response is to urge people to read the book through and to see if it works. But I admit, secondly, that there are still some matters of principle that are worth discussing at length, though this is not quite the place to do it. I might have to write something elsewhere to respond to these issues.

I would like to point out, finally, that since this was first published I have written a companion volume, *Light to Live by* (Quaker Books 2002), which describes my attempts to put Fox's 'experiment with light' into practice.

Rex Ambler, Silverdale, 2006.

VI   *Truth of the heart*

INTRODUCTION

This collection of passages from the writings of George Fox (1624-1691) is meant to do two things: to make available his clearest and most profound writings from the whole range of his works, and to display them in such a way as to show the connections between them. It should therefore be possible in reading the text through to gain a picture of Fox's whole vision.

This may at first seem like a rather cumbersome device for conveying Fox's meaning. Why not simply publish some of his more interesting work? The reason is that he nowhere set out his ideas as a whole, systematically. His writing (or dictating, as was usually the case) was nearly always occasional, responding to a particular situation and with the particular inspiration that came to him. Indeed, he wrote, it seems, *as* the inspiration came to him, without forethought or working over afterwards. He lacked the education and the inclination to structure his thoughts rationally. There is therefore much repetition, digression and even confusion in his thought. He also developed the habit, especially in his later work, of letting the Bible do the talking for him, but without stopping to explain precisely how he interpreted the Bible in these cases. Explanation and clarification were not his strong points, which is surprising in a teacher of such profound influence. But for all this, there are times when he wrote with extraordinary clarity, depth and power, presenting an understanding of life that was both coherent and livable. How else then could this writing be made available than by collecting all the bits together and putting them in an order that would reflect Fox's own intentions? What is surprising is that something like it has never been done before. The greater part of his work has therefore remained in obscurity, difficult to find in the few libraries that keep the old works, and difficult to read when the old works have finally been tracked down. Does this mean, I ask myself, that we have remained in ignorance of Fox's wider vision for more than three hundred years?

We have always had Fox's Journal, of course. But this impressive work was not intended as a vehicle of his teaching. It was written, as he says himself, 'that all may know the dealings of the Lord with me... to prepare and fit me for the work unto which he had appointed me'.[1] It is an account of his activities, often with the intention of showing how he had been guided to do what he did, or vindicated by events in doing it. It has a defensive tone, perhaps because, at the time of writing (mostly in 1676), he was burdened by the sufferings that Friends were having to undergo for their witness. If we depend on this document for an understanding of Fox's teaching, we shall get a confused and unedifying picture. This is no doubt the reason why the first editor of the Journal, Thomas Ellwood, included a number of papers and epistles that Fox had written earlier, in the 25 years before he wrote the Journal, because there Fox wrote mostly with clarity and force about the issues that concerned him. Unfortunately, those papers were not included in later editions, such as the scholarly edition of John Nickalls. And we have little else in print, in Britain at least, to give us access to that early teaching.[2]

I had to go out of my way to discover what else Fox had written. I was soon pleased to find, however, that the collected *Works* of 1831 had just been reprinted by the George Fox Fund in America.[3] There were eight large volumes, two of which were the Ellwood edition of the Journal, with the additional early papers included. There were also two volumes of epistles, an almost complete col-

lection, and three volumes of 'doctrinals', including some important early tracts from the 1650s, when the Quaker movement
began. These I read from beginning to end, to get a sense of Fox's
vision as a whole, and to see what I'd been missing in reading
only the Journal.

There was a lot. In the epistles especially – open letters, as we
would call them, or letters to groups of people – there was a great
deal of advice on the spiritual life which amplified and clarified his
message considerably. Already in the first 20 epistles I discovered
something which changed my whole understanding of what Fox
was trying to do. I had always had the impression that Fox had a
doctrine that there was 'that of God in everyone' and that he went
around the country trying to persuade people to believe this. The
doctrine, as I understood it, was essentially a mystical one, but he
clothed it in the biblical and Christian language of his day. He could
therefore *sound* like a puritan preacher, or even like a modern-day
evangelical, but his intention was something quite different: to
bring people to an essentially wordless experience of union with
God. I was influenced here by the two prevalent understandings
of his mission, which rather opposed one another, the mystical
view of Rufus Jones and what I thought of as the 'protestant' view
of Lewis Benson. I was simply trying to reconcile them in my own
way of thinking. But a close reading of the text now convinced me
that I was quite off the mark. I now saw that Fox had a distinctive
approach of his own, which was not consciously drawing on any
of the traditions he inherited. He was not, for example, presenting
a teaching that people were expected to believe and follow,
whether mystical, biblical or whatever. He was telling them rather
to do something, because what they needed to make them free and
fulfilled as human beings, 'perfect', was in them, and it was in them
already without their having to imbibe it from a church or teaching outside. It was an inner awareness which would enable them
initially 'to see themselves' as they were, in reality, beyond the

deceptions of 'the self', but then also to see what they and others could become, and should become. It was a powerful and transforming 'light', and it worked its magic in people by showing them 'the truth'.

That, essentially, was it. I was astonished at its simplicity, and also its originality, given the environment in which it appeared. In one move this teaching undercut the established religion of authority, whether Protestant or Catholic. By pointing to a resource within people it in effect challenged everyone to find their own inner truth, and to learn to trust it and live by it. And by encouraging people to *act* on what they saw in the light, it grounded their faith in everyday life, avoiding the withdrawals of classical mysticism. There was however a discipline here, despite its liberating tendency. For the light had first of all to be discovered, since it was generally smothered by the more self-centred activities of the mind, such as thinking and imagining. And once discovered, by a discipline of waiting in silence, it had to be attended to and adhered to, if its power was to be felt. There was in fact, for both individual and group, a distinct *process* to be undergone. This became apparent as I read advice such as the following, from an early tract of 1653, 'The first step to peace is to stand still in the light', suggesting there would be a second step, and possibly a third, and from an epistle of 1652, 'Stand still in that which is pure, after ye see yourselves; and then mercy comes in. After thou seest thy thoughts, and the temptations, do not think, submit; and then power comes in'. (These are included in the Anthology, in 1:89 and 1:90 respectively; the numbers indicate part one, extracts 89 and 90, which are the numbers at the beginning of the extract, referring to the endnotes. This system for referring to extracts will be used throughout the Anthology.) These steps were recommended, it seems, almost in the manner of a scientific experiment. If people then did what Fox urged them to do, they would discover for themselves the validity of what he and other Friends said. They would know the truth 'experimentally' (1:13).

Part of my enthusiasm for this unique spirituality was a sense of its relevance to my own situation, and to that of many other people like me. So in order, among other things, to understand it better I tried to put it into practice over a number of years.[4] The result of that 'experiment' was that I not only came to understand Fox a lot better, but I also came to see how that understanding could be worked out today. In the way I have described it so far I have already undertaken a translation into the language of my own time, suggesting that my recognition of what Fox was doing was at the same time a recognition of what could be done now, in a situation obviously very different from his.

Having discovered all this in the epistles and tracts of the first three or four years of his movement, I was eager then to discover if this was continued in later writings. So I read the *Works* systematically over a period of two years, marking all those passages that struck me for their clarity and depth, then listing the reference under one of his key words, such as 'truth', 'power', 'life', 'light' (these four, as it happens, are the most frequent in his writing). I had thought initially that this would be enough, but by the time I finished I was aware that something else had to be done. There were well over 300 references, and within each section as I had devised it ('truth', 'light' and so on) there was a subtle complexity that was becoming increasingly obvious: 'the light', for example, revealed the truth progressively, beginning with 'sin and evil' in people, but then moving on to new possibilities represented by 'the seed' in people, which produced new 'life'. How could I explore these subtle relationships? I decided on the laborious device of typing up all the marked passages on to my computer so that I could see them directly in relation to one another, and also play around with them to see if there was any natural order in which they might appear. The best clue to this, I found, was the sense I had gained at the beginning of the enquiry of a process that had to be undergone, and of the insights that are acquired, in sequence as it were, in following that process. But the nature of that process also became clearer: there was, for example, a process for the group, 'the meeting', as well as a process for the individual, and there was, thirdly, another process for the world, or rather a process of interaction with the world. These three seemed to run in parallel, mirroring each other, but also interacting with each other. 'Mind the light, that all may be refreshed one in another, and all in one' (2:3). 'From the truth floweth justice, equity, righteousness and godliness, mercy and tenderness, that brings a man's heart, mind, soul and spirit to the infinite and incomprehensible God, and from it a love flows to all the universal creation' (3:84).

I therefore used the pattern of thinking I discerned in Fox to arrange the texts. There was nothing awkward about this, as it turned out; the texts fell into place naturally, as if they belonged there. What is more, they seemed to connect with each other, as if to form a continuous narrative. When I read through the collection for the first time I was greatly surprised, and delighted, by the way it all cohered, and by its sense of an unfolding vision. What I was reading was new, I felt, as if this vision of life had never actually been articulated before, which in a sense is true. At any rate, you could say it was the kind of systematic book we might wish Fox himself had written, and a book that he could have written if he had been minded to do so.

At that point I realised the collection might be worth publishing, just as it stood, and not be left simply as a database for my own private use. In fact, it occurred to me that it *ought* to be published, whether I liked the idea or not, because this was now a resource that no one who took Fox seriously could afford to be without.

Also, it didn't seem to need commentary, other than the introductory remarks I am making here. It spoke for itself. The different texts, difficult though some of them were, interpreted one another. It would, no doubt, take more than one reading to get a sense of

the thing as a whole, and it might need some paraphrasing, trans-
lating into modern English, and cross-referencing from one end
to the other, but the resources for understanding all seemed to be
there. I therefore decided to present the text exactly as I wrote it
up for myself.

Since making that decision, however, I have had to change my
opinion somewhat. When I showed the text to a number of friends
to try it out on them, their comments and questions indicated to
me that it did after all need some commentary. I had obviously
taken for granted the many hours I had spent reading Fox and the
writers around him and so didn't anticipate the difficulty others
would have when they came to Fox for the very first time, or even
the second and third time. There are therefore now four resources
added to the text which should help people to understand it. One
is the references to the Bible in the endnotes. Fox's first readers
would no doubt have recognised his biblical allusions immediately,
but we generally would not. The references are therefore intended
to help in understanding Fox. They are not intended, I should add,
to provide some kind of authorisation for what he was saying, or
to suggest that Fox himself was implicitly quoting the Bible as an
authority. As will be clear from the Anthology itself (e.g. 2:44-49)
he made use of the Bible to articulate his own insights, seeing it s
inspired by the same spirit that was now inspiring him, and inspiring many others too. So I have given a reference to a passage when,
and only when, I thought it would add to our understanding of it.

Another resource is the Glossary at the end of the text, describing the meaning (for Fox) of some 100 words which would have
a different meaning for us more than three hundred years later, or
perhaps no meaning at all. Certain words of his are loaded with
theological meaning, which we need to grasp very clearly if we
are not to invest them too quickly with meanings of our own.
Words such as 'Christ', 'spirit', 'sin', 'truth' had a specific meaning
for him which is rather different from the meaning that people

today are most likely to attach to them.

Thirdly, for the sake initially of Friends in Europe for whom English was at best a second language, there is a translation of the whole text into modern English. I have tried first of all to make the meaning clear and accessible to a modern reader, as clear at any rate as the original would have been to Fox's first readers. For this reason I have not always succeeded in conveying the richness of the original, especially the allusions to the Bible, though where that was important I have added a biblical reference in the text or even quoted the Bible directly. Where I have quoted or picked up an allusion to the Bible I have normally used the Revised English Bible, which I have also taken as something of a model in clear translation. One or two phrases baffled me, I have to say, e.g. 'Though ye swell in venom' (1:1) and 'keep your habitations' (1:125, 2:91). I hope my guesses were inspired. For the most part, though, I am confident that I got it right.

Finally, there is an essay on Fox which tries to make sense of his teaching as a whole, linking the various themes of the Anthology.

So it turns out that there is a commentary after all, but not one, I hope, that prevents people from drawing further meaning from the text or exploring its meaning for their own life and thought. In any case, no commentary could define its meaning once and for all, for what is being expressed here is an experiential approach to truth which can really be understood only by entering into the experience itself. So the text in its new form now stands, again, as it did in Fox's day, as a warning against ready-made interpretations of life and as an invitation to experiment with truth in our own life and experience.[5]

I should add a note here about the editing of the text. I have modernised the spelling and punctuation, for the sake of readability, but otherwise I have left the text exactly as it was. One or two extracts are given more than once, when they seemed to contribute to more than one theme, and some extracts are included simply because they help to make a connection in the unravelling of a theme, or explain Fox's thinking or use of a word, even though they add little or nothing of depth to it.

Rex Ambler, Birmingham 2001

ENDNOTES for introduction

1. This is the opening statement of the Journal: see e.g. John Nickalls' edition, OUP, 1952, p.1.
2. The little that we have is to be found mostly in Cecil Sharman's publication of a few of the epistles in *No more but my love* (Quaker Home Service, London, 1980), John Lampen's *Wait in the Light: the spirituality of George Fox* (Quaker Home Service, London, 1981) and Hugh MacGregor Ross's *George Fox speaks for himself* (Sessions, York, 1991), which prints some previously unpublished writings of Fox. In America, however, there is not only T. Canby Jones' edition of the epistles, which selects from all of them, *The power of the Lord is over all* (Friends United Press, Richmond, Indiana, 1989), but there is also the reprint of the 1831 edition of the collected *Works of George Fox* (New Foundation Publication, George Fox Fund, State College, Pennsylvania, 1991) in eight large volumes.
3. See note above.
4. I have written on these experiments and the understanding that came of them in *Light to Live by*, Quaker Books, London, 2002.
5. I have written more fully on early Quaker spirituality in 'The discipline of light' in *The Presence in the midst* (Quaker Theology Seminar, 1996); 'Quaker truth' in *Authority and tradition* (Quaker

Theology Seminar, 1997); and 'Quaker identity' in The Friends
Quarterly (October 1997). This material should appear with
other essays for the Quaker Theology Seminar in my next book
in prepration, Quaker Truth. For those who would like to explore
the history behind it I would recommend Hugh Barbour, The
Quakers in Puritan England (Friends United Press, Richmond,
Indiana, 1985), Hugh Barbour and J. William Frost, The Quakers
(Friends United Press, Richmond, Indiana, 1994), H. Larry
Ingle, First among Friends: George Fox and the creation of Quakerism
(Oxford University Press, 1994), and Rosemary Moore, The
Light in their consciences: the early Quakers in Britain, 1646-1666 (Penn-
sylvania State University Press, 2000). A new edition of Fox's
Journal has just been made available, edited by Nigel Smith and
published in 1998 in Penguin Classics. All these can be
obtained from The Quaker Bookshop, Friends House, 173
Euston Road, London NW1 2BJ, tel. 020 7663 1030.
www.quaker.org.uk / www.mph.org.uk

ACKNOWLEDGEMENTS

I want to express my gratitude for the inspiration
of Joseph Pickvance: he was the first person to make
me aware that Fox was still important. I think he would
have liked this book. My gratitude also to Neil Sawyer
and Sima Gonsai who helped with the typing – a
labour of love – and to Doug Gwyn for
help on the interpretive essay.

ANTHOLOGY
part 1: *the individual*

THE MISSION

1 Consider, O people who are within the parish of Ulverston, I was moved of the Lord to come into your public places to speak among you, being sent of God to direct your minds to him, that you might know where to find your teacher; that your minds might be stayed alone upon God, and you might not gad abroad without you for a teacher; for the Lord God alone will teach his people; he is coming to teach them, and to gather his people from idols' temples, and from the customary worships which all the world is trained up in. And God hath given to every one of you a measure of his spirit according to your capacity; liars, drunkards, whoremongers, and thieves, and who follow filthy pleasures, you all have this measure in you. And this is the measure of the spirit of God that shows you sin, evil, and deceit; which lets you see lying is sin; theft, drunkenness, and uncleanness, to be the works of darkness. Therefore mind your measure… and prize your time while you have it, lest the time come that you will say, with sorrow, we had time, but it is past. O, why will ye die? Why will ye choose your own ways? Why will ye follow the course of the world? Know ye not in your consciences, that all these are evil and sin? And that such as act these things shall never enter into the kingdom of God? O, that ye would consider and see how you have spent your time, and mind how ye spend your time, and observe whom ye serve; for the wages of sin is death. Do not ye know, that whatsoever is more than yea and nay cometh of evil?… Though ye swell in venom, and live in lust for awhile, yet God will find you out, and bring you to judgment. Therefore love the light which Christ hath enlightened you withal, who saith, I am the light of the world, and who enlightens every one that cometh into the world.

THE MISSION

1 Think of this you people of Ulverston. The reason I came to your public places to speak among you was that I was moved by the Lord to do so. I was sent by God to direct your minds to him, so that you would know where to find your teacher. And being able to rest your minds on God you would not then have to run around looking elsewhere for a teacher: the Lord God alone will teach his people. And he is coming to teach them, and to gather his people out of temples devoted to idols, and away from the customary religious practices that they have all been trained in. And God has given to every one of you a portion of his spirit according to your capacity. Even those of you who habitually lie, get drunk, go to prostitutes, steal other people's goods and seek unwholesome pleasures, you all have this portion in you. In fact it is this that shows you that you are doing wrong. It is this that makes you aware that lying is wrong, that theft, drunkenness and anything unwholesome come out of the darkness of ignorance. Therefore pay attention to it, this gift you have... and value your time while you still have it, in case the time comes when you say, with sorrow, we had time but it's gone.

Oh, why do you want to die? Why do you insist on choosing your own way? Why do you want to do just what everybody else is doing? Don't you realise in your conscience that all these things are wrong? And that people who do these things will never enter the kingdom of God? If only you would stop and think what you've been doing with your time, and what you're doing with it now, and observe who it is in all this that you're working for; for those who 'work for sin... get death for their wages' (Romans 6:23)!

Don't you realise that when you can't be satisfied with a simple yes or no evil has already begun?... Though now you vent your spleen and give way to your lust, eventually God will find you out and bring you to account. Therefore cherish the light that Christ has enlightened you with. Christ said, 'I am the light of the world', and he enlightens every-

Therefore to the light in you I speak; and when the book of conscience shall come to be opened, then shall you witness what I say to be true, and you all shall be judged out of it. So God Almighty direct your minds (such of you especially as love honesty and sincerity), that you may receive mercy in the time of need. Your teacher is within you; look not forth: it will teach you, both lying in bed and going abroad, to shun all occasion of sin and evil.

2 This message of the glorious, everlasting gospel was I sent forth to declare and publish, and thousands by it are turned to God, having received it.... And since I have declared this message in this part of the world and in America, and have written books of the same, to spread it universally abroad, the blind prophets, preachers and deceivers have given over telling us, the false prophets should 'come in the last times'; for a great light is sprung up and shines over their heads: so that every child in truth sees the folly of their sayings.

3 For the God of power, light and glory hath raised up a light in his people, and gathered their hearts together to himself, and hath discovered unto them the vanity of all things wherein they have lived, and showed them his way and truth, where they should walk and glorify him, and serve him in holiness and newness of life; and with eternal food, the bread of life, doth he feed us, whereby we become wonders to the world, and as he hath raised his seed to his praise and glory, and is adding daily to his church, and the strong man bows himself, and the keepers of the house tremble, and the powers of the earth shake, and the glory of the Lord is rising, and is risen, which terribly shakes the earth, that the idols of gold and silver are cast away, and God alone loved, who is Lord of heaven and earth; and the works of the Lord are strange and wondrous, as ever were, as the scriptures witness.

one who comes into the world.

So it is the light in you that I'm speaking to. And when the Book of Conscience comes to be opened you will see for yourselves that what I say is true. And that is how you will all be judged. So may God Almighty direct your minds – those of you especially who love honesty and sincerity – that you may receive mercy in your time of need. Your teacher is inside you, don't look outside. And it will teach you wherever you are, lying in bed or going out and about, to avoid everything that leads you to do wrong.

2 This message of the glorious, everlasting gospel I was sent out to declare and publish, and thousands have received it and been turned to God by it.... And since I have declared this message in this part of the world and in America, and written books about it to spread it as widely as possible, the blind prophets, preachers and deceivers have given up telling us that the false prophets 'should be expected to come in the last times'. For a great light has sprung up and shines over their heads so that every child in truth can see the folly of what they say.

3 For the God of power, light and glory has raised up a light in his people and gathered their hearts together to himself. And he has revealed to them the emptiness of everything their lives have been based on, and shown them his way and truth, where they should walk and glorify him and serve him in a new and holy life. And he feeds us with eternal food, the bread of life. As a result of all this we have become wonders to the world. He has raised a seed [in us] to bring him praise and glory, and he is adding daily to his church, and 'the strong man bows down' and 'the keepers of the house tremble' (Ecclesiastes 12:3) and 'the powers of the earth shake', and the glory of the Lord is rising and has risen, which shakes the earth terribly. So the idols of gold and silver are thrown away and only God is loved, the Lord of heaven and earth (Isaiah 2:17-21). The actions of the Lord are strange and wonderful, as they always were, and as the scriptures bear witness.

FALSE RELIGION

4 Yet you in your darkness will go make an image of God, of the bigness of a corruptible man. When you are not able to comprehend him, the incomprehensible God, the omnipotent God, who is invisible and omnipotent, forbids you to make an image of him. And is there any image that you make but you do adore in your hearts or applaud or delight in, when all images are utterly forbidden to be made by the Lord, who is in all and over all? And all nations are but as the drop of a bucket before him, who measures the waters as in the hollow of his hand, and comprehends the dust of the earth as in a measure, etc. Yet silly man in his foolish imagination will go make an image of him.... And you make images of God like yourselves. So are you not far degenerated by your foolishness and ignorance from the spirit and truth of him in yourselves, in your own hearts, who is to be reverenced, honoured, worshipped, obeyed and served in all things, by his power and in his spirit?

Yet you poor silly creatures, empty of life or light or grace or truth which comes from the God of truth, to have your image makers make an image of him who the heaven of heavens is not able to contain, the heaven also being his throne and the earth his footstool, and who fills the heaven and the earth. And yet you in your foolishness, darkness and ignorance go make an image of the incomprehensible God, and so you will comprehend him in the fashion of a man.

5 And why have they so many religions? Because they are out of the pure and undefiled religion before God, which was set up above sixteen hundred years ago... and they are gone from this religion, into those of their own making, and tell people, they must not be perfect here, and must carry a body of death with them to the grave.

6 They speak a divination of their own brain, and not from the mouth of the Lord.

FALSE RELIGION

4 Yet you in your ignorance want to make an image of God, of the size of a corruptible human being. When you find that you are unable to comprehend this God who is indeed incomprehensible, then the omnipotent God, who is invisible, forbids you to make an image of him. And is there any image that you make that you do not adore in your hearts or applaud or take delight in? Yet all constructed images are absolutely forbidden by the Lord, who is in all and over all.

All nations are but a drop in the bucket before the one who measures the seas in the hollow of his hand and contains the dust of the earth as in a measuring bowl. Yet silly humans in their foolish imagination try to make an image of him.... And you make images of God to look just like you! Have you fallen so far in your foolishness and ignorance from his spirit and truth in yourselves, in your own hearts, from the one who is to be revered, honoured, worshipped, obeyed and served in all things, by his power and in his spirit?

You are such poor, silly creatures, bereft of life or light or grace or truth – which comes from the God of truth – that you have to have image makers make you an image of him whom even the heaven of heavens cannot contain. The heaven is also his throne and the earth his footstool, and he fills the heaven and the earth. And yet you in your foolishness, darkness and ignorance go and make an image of the incomprehensible God, and in this way you try to comprehend him on the model of a human being.

5 And why do they have so many religions? Because they have abandoned the religion that is pure and untarnished before God, that was set up more than sixteen hundred years ago... and they have left this religion for those of their own making, and they tell people they cannot be perfect in this life and must carry 'a body of death' with them to the grave.

6 They speak a divination of their own brain, and not from the mouth of the Lord.

7 Silence all presumptuous talkers of God, who see him not.

8 And you that do profess the primitive, pure, and undefiled religion, which is above all the religions in the world, show it forth in life and practice.

9 None can live the life of the true christians, and the holy prophets and apostles, except they are in the same power and spirit, grace and truth, and faith and image that they were in.

10 While people's minds do run in the earthly, after the creatures and changeable things, and changeable ways and religions, and changeable, uncertain teachers, their minds are in bondage. And they are brittle and changeable, and tossed up and down with windy doctrines and thoughts, and notions and things, their minds being from the unchangeable truth in the inward parts, the light of Jesus Christ, which would keep their minds to the unchangeable, who is the way to the Father.

11 The mighty day of the Lord is come, and coming, wherein all hearts shall be made manifest, and the secrets of everyone's heart shall be revealed by the light of Jesus, who lighteth every man that cometh into the world.

12 Now you have time prize it; this is the day of your visitation.

EXPERIENCE

13 As I had forsaken the priests, so I left the separate preachers also, and those called the most experienced people; for I saw there was none among them all that could speak to my condition. And when all my hopes in them and in all men were gone, so that I had nothing outwardly to help me, nor could tell what to do; then, O then I heard a voice which said, 'There is one, even Christ Jesus, that can

7 You have the presumption to talk about God when you are not even aware of him? Silence, I tell you!

8 And you who do profess the original, pure and untarnished religion, which is above all the religions of the world, show it in your life and practice.

9 No one can live the life of the true Christians, the life of the holy prophets and apostles, unless they live by the same power and spirit, grace and truth and faith that they lived by.

10 So long as people's minds are involved with material things, with things that have been made and are therefore liable to change, and so long as they are involved with religions and ways of life that are similarly changeable, and with unreliable teachers, their minds are enslaved. And they are insecure and unstable, tossed up and down with windy doctrines and thoughts, ideas and things, for their minds have abandoned the dependable truth in their own inner being, the light of Jesus Christ, who would keep their minds on what cannot be changed, who is indeed the way to the Father.

11 The great day of the Lord has come and is coming when every heart will be disclosed and the secrets of everyone's heart will be revealed by the light of Jesus, who enlightens everyone who comes into the world.

12 Now you have time value it; this is your day of opportunity, given you by God.

EXPERIENCE

13 Just as I gave up on the priests, I left the 'separate' preachers also, and those called 'the most experienced people', for I could see that there was no one among them who could speak to me as I was. And when all my hopes in them and in all human beings were gone, so that I had nothing outside me to help me or tell me what to do, then, oh then I heard a voice which said, 'There is someone, Christ Jesus, who speak to thy condition'. When I heard it, my heart did leap for joy. Then the Lord let me see why there was none upon the earth that could speak to my condition, namely, that I might give him all the glory.... Jesus Christ... enlightens, and gives grace, faith, and power. Thus when God doth work, who shall let it? This I knew experimentally.

14   This I know by experience and therefore it is good to trust in the Lord.

15   All must first know the voice crying in the wilderness, in their hearts.

16   As there is a world without you, so there is a world in the heart.

17   All keep in the sense of truth, and be digging for the pearl in your own field, and to find the silver in your own house.

18   I have examined myself and proved myself, and have found Christ Jesus in me.

19   Is it not more of honour and credit to prove all things and try all things?

20   Therefore come forth and let it be tried, for this would bring glory to God and the truth to be manifest, for much blood had been shed about these things, as in Queen Mary's days.

21   Let your faith be in the power that goes through all things, and over all things, and every one hearken to it. So the power of the mighty God know (the arm), and how it works, and the hand how it carries you, which brings out of tribulation... into peace.

22   Come ye captives out of prison, and rejoice with one

can speak to you as you are'. When I heard this, my heart leapt for joy. Then the Lord let me see why there was no one on earth who could speak to me as I was: so that I might give him all the credit....

Jesus Christ... enlightens and gives grace, faith and power. So when God works like this, who can stop him? This I knew to be true from experience.

14 This I know by experience and therefore it is good to trust in the Lord.

15 Everyone must first of all get to know 'the voice crying in the wilderness', in their hearts.

16 Just as there is a world outside you, so there is also a world in the heart.

17 All of you stay aware of truth, and keep digging for the pearl in your own field, and looking for the silver in your own house.

18 I have examined myself and tested myself and found Christ Jesus in me.

19 Doesn't it do more honour and credit to try everything and test everything?

20 So come forward and let it be put to the test, for this is the way to bring glory to God and make the truth evident, for much blood has been shed over these things, as in the days of Queen Mary.

21 Let your faith be in the power that activates everything, and transcends it too, and every one of you pay attention to it. Get to know the power of the mighty God, 'the arm of God', and how it works, and get to know 'the hand of God' and how it carries you, how it brings you out of trouble... into peace.

22 Come out of prison all you who have been held there, and rejoice

accord, for the joyful days are coming. Let us be glad, and rejoice for ever! Singleness of heart is come; pureness of heart is come; joy and gladness are come.

INWARDNESS

23 Keep within. And when they shall say, 'lo here', or 'lo there is Christ', go not forth; for Christ is within you. And they are seducers and antichrists which draw your minds out from the teaching within you. For the measure is within, and the light of God is within, and the pearl is within you, which is hid; and the word of God is within you, and ye are the temples of God; and God hath said, he will dwell in you and walk in you. And then what need ye go to the idols' temples without you?

24 These things ye must all find within, there is your peace, and there refreshing comes into your souls from the Lord.

25 The Lord showed me, that the natures of those things which were hurtful without, were within in the hearts and minds of wicked men. The natures of dogs, swine, vipers… etc. The natures of these I saw within, though people had been looking without.

26   But to speak of these things being within, seemed strange to the rough, crooked, and mountainous ones.

27 I saw the state of those, both priests and people, who, in reading the scriptures, cry out much against Cain, Esau, Judas and other wicked men of former times mentioned in the holy scriptures, but do not see the nature of Cain, of Esau, of Judas and those others, in themselves. These said it was they, they, they that were the bad people, putting it off from themselves, but when some of these came, with the light and spirit of truth, to see into themselves, then they came to say, I, I, I, it is I myself that have been the Ishmael, the Esau, etc…. When these, who were so much taken up

together, for the days of joy are coming. Let's be glad and rejoice for ever! Sincerity of heart has come. Purity of heart has come. Joy and gladness have come.

INWARDNESS

23 Stay inside. And when they say, 'Look here', or 'Look there is Christ', don't go out there, for Christ is inside you. And those who try to seduce you and draw your minds away from the teaching inside you are opposed to Christ. For the portion is inside, the light of God is inside, and the pearl is inside, though hidden. And the word of God is inside you, and you are the temples of God, and God has said he will make his home in you and walk with you. So why go to the temples of idols outside you?

24 These things you must all find inside, there is your peace and there comes refreshment to your souls from the Lord.

25 The Lord showed me that the things that cause hurt externally are themselves internal, in the hearts and minds of wicked people. [E.g. when they call other people names such as] 'dogs', 'swine', 'vipers'… etc. The cause of these hurts I saw within, though people had been looking outside themselves.

26 But to speak of these things being within seemed strange to those who take the rough, crooked and mountainous road.

27 I could see what they were doing, these priests and their people, when they read the scriptures and [vehemently] denounced Cain, Esau, Judas and other wicked people of the past mentioned in the holy scriptures. They were failing to see the characteristics of Cain, Esau, Judas and the others in themselves. These people would say it was 'they, they, they' that were the bad people, putting it off from themselves. But when, with the help of the light and the spirit of truth, some of them came to see into themselves, then they came to say 'I, I, I, it is I myself that have been the Ishmael, the Esau, etc'. When these with finding fault with others and thought themselves clear from these things, came to look into themselves and with the light of Christ thoroughly to search themselves, they might see enough of this in themselves; then the cry could not be it is he or they, but I and we are found in these conditions.

28 We need no mass to teach us, for the spirit that gave forth the scripture teacheth us how to pray, sing, praise, rejoice, honour and worship God, and in what, and how to walk and to behave ourselves to God and man, and leadeth us into all truth, in which is our unity; and it is our comforter and guide and leader, and not men without who say they have not the spirit and power that the apostles had.

29 You, that deny the light which lighteth every man that cometh into the world, are seduced from the anointing which should teach you; and if ye would be taught by it, ye would not need that any man should teach you.

30 Every man, every woman then must come to the spirit of God in their own selves; for it will give them understanding and knowledge, and give them instruction, it will help their infirmities, it will let them see their wants.

31 When the woman of Samaria came out to fetch water at Jacob's well, the woman reasoned with Christ about worship, and she said, 'Our fathers worshipped at this mountain, but others at Jerusalem;' and Christ answered her again, 'The time cometh that neither at Jerusalem nor at this mountain shall God be worshipped'. There he denied the continuance of these two public places of worship; and when he had done that, he set up another worship, for he said, 'God was a spirit, and they that worshipped him must worship him in the spirit and in the truth; for the hour cometh, and now is, that such God seeks to worship him'.... And is not the spirit within, and the truth in the

people, who were so much taken up with finding fault with others and thought themselves clear of these things, came to look into themselves and with the light of Christ thoroughly to search themselves, they would see quite enough of these things in their own lives. Then the cry could not be 'it is he or they', but 'I and we are found in this condition'.

28 We don't need a mass to teach us, because the spirit that gave us the scripture teaches us. It teaches us how to pray, sing, praise, rejoice, honour and worship God, and how to live and behave towards God and other people. It leads us to all the truth [we need to know], which is where we find our unity, and it is our comforter and guide and leader. It is the spirit that does all this, and not human beings out there who don't even claim to have the spirit and the power that the apostles had.

29 You who deny that there is a light that enlightens everyone who comes into the world, you are being seduced from the one who could empower you and teach you. And if you allowed yourselves to be taught by it, you would not then need a human being to teach you.

30 Every man, every woman then must come to the spirit of God in their own selves, for it is this that will give them understanding and knowledge, and give them instruction. It will help them in their weakness. It will let them see their needs.

31 When the woman of Samaria came out to fetch water at Jacob's Well, the woman reasoned with Christ about worship, and she said, 'Our fathers used to worship on this mountain, but others in Jerusalem'. And Christ answered her again, 'The time is coming when God will be worshipped neither in Jerusalem nor on this mountain'. He insisted there that these two places of worship could not continue, and having done that he then set up another kind of worship, for he said, 'God is a spirit, and those who worship him must worship him in the spirit and in the truth, for the hour is coming and has already arrived when God looks for people to

inward parts?... And can any worship God who is a spirit, in the truth, but they must come to the spirit and the truth of God in their own hearts?

32 Now where is this spirit, and where is this truth? Is it not within people?... And so every man and woman in the whole world must come to the spirit and truth in their own hearts, by which they must know the God of truth.

TRUTH

33 They must be in it, and in the truth, to worship the God of all truth.

34 Every one is to be in it, and to walk in the truth, and in the spirit, and to come to the truth in their own particulars.... And so none can worship the God of truth, but who come to the truth in their own hearts.

35 Love the truth more than all.

36 Loathe deceit and all unrighteousness, hard-heartedness, wronging, cozening, cheating, or unjust dealing; but live and reign in the righteous life and power of God and wisdom... doing truth to all, without respect to persons; to high or low whatsoever, young or old, rich or poor.... Let truth be the head and practise it.

37 If you want wisdom, keep in the truth, that you may go to the treasure of life and of salvation.... For the truth is the truth, and changeth not, in which live, and it will be your peace and joy everlasting.

38 You are to buy the truth and not sell it; and truth is that that is stronger than all.

39 Truth is that which is pure...; for the way being the truth, is

worship him like this'.... And isn't the spirit inside, and the truth in one's own inner being?... And can anyone worship God who is a spirit, in the truth, if they don't come to the spirit and truth of God in their own hearts?

32 Now where is this spirit, and where is this truth? Aren't they inside people?... So every man and woman in the whole world must come to the spirit and truth in their own hearts, for this is the way they will come to know the God of truth.

TRUTH

33 They must be in [the spirit], and in the truth, to worship the God of all truth.

34 Everyone is to be in [the truth] and live their lives in the truth, and to come to the truth in their own personal experience.... And so no one can worship the God of truth if they don't come to the truth in their own hearts.

35 Love the truth more than anything.

36 Loathe deceit and every kind of injustice: hard-heartedness, betrayal, fraud, cheating and unfair dealing. But live with freedom in the life and power of God which will enable you to do the right thing and to act wisely... acting according to truth in relation to everyone you meet, high or low, young or old, rich or poor.... Let truth be your first concern and put it into practice.

37 If you lack wisdom stay with the truth. In this way you will find the treasure of life and salvation.... For the truth is the truth and doesn't change. Live in it and it will be your everlasting peace and joy.

38 You should buy the truth and not sell it. And there is nothing stronger than truth.

the same as it was in the beginning, though many things have risen against it: yet it remains the same pure truth, and holy way.

40 In the truth live, which the devil and his works are out of; and that truth makes you free.

41 And if the truth make you free, then are ye free indeed... free from all the will-worships, and from all the windy doctrines; from all the evil inventions, traditions, imaginations, and notions, and rudiments of Adam in the fall.

42 And all my dear friends, be faithful, and quench not the spirit, but be obedient to the truth, and spread it abroad, which must go over all the world, to professors, Jews, christians, and heathen, to the answering the witness of God in them all; that they may come to the truth, which answers the witness in them, to be made free by it.

43 Be not amazed at the weather.... Though the waves and storms be high, yet your faith will keep you to swim above them, for they are but for a time, and the truth is without time.... And do not think that anything will outlast the truth, which standeth sure... for the good will overcome the evil; and the light darkness; and the life death.... The false prophet cannot overcome the true, but the true prophet Christ will overcome all the false. So be faithful, and live in that which doth not think the time long.

44 Blessed be the Lord, the truth is reached in the hearts of people beyond words.

DECEIT

45 When once you deny the truth then you are given over to believe lies.... O, therefore, tremble before the Lord ye hypocrites, and mind the light of God in you, which shows you the deceit of your hearts, and obey that.

39 Truth is what is pure…; for since the way to life is truth it is the same as it was in the beginning. Though many things have risen to oppose it, it remains the same pure truth and holy way.

40 If you live in truth, which the devil has abandoned in everything he has done, then that truth will set you free.

41 And if the truth sets you free, you are indeed free… free from all ego-based religion, and free from all the airy doctrines, from all the hurtful inventions, traditions, contrived images, ideas and principles of fallen human beings.

42 And all my dear friends, be faithful, and do not stifle the spirit, but be obedient to the truth and spread it about widely. This truth has to be taken across the world to everyone who professes faith – Jews, Christians, heathen – so that it will echo the witness of God they all have in them and that they in turn will come to the truth that resonates within them, and be set free by it.

43 Don't be surprised at the weather…. Though the waves and storms are high, your faith will enable you to swim above them. They are only here for a time, but the truth is outside time…. And don't imagine that anything will outlast the truth, for it stands secure… the good will overcome the evil, and the light darkness, and the life death…. The false prophet cannot overcome the true one, but the true prophet Christ will overcome the false one. So be faithful, and live in that reality for which the time is never too long.

44 Blessed be the Lord, the truth in people's hearts has been reached, beyond words.

DECEIT

45 Once you deny the truth you are forced to believe lies…. So, tremble

46 The devil abode not in the truth. So the Jews were called 'of the devil' when they went out of the truth.... And there is no promise of God to the devil that ever he shall return into truth again. But the promise of God is to man and woman, that have been deceived by him.... And much more was opened concerning these things which will be too large to speak of.

47 The Ranters pleaded that God made the devil, but I denied it and I told them... he became a devil by going out of truth and so became a murderer and a destroyer. And so I showed them that God did not make the devil, for God is a God of truth and made all things good and blessed them.

48 The serpent... that led man from God, who is the prince of the world, the prince of darkness, and... the father of lies, a murderer from the beginning, the corrupter of mankind, the author of the separation from God, and the original of sin, the beginning of it.

49 Every one keep on their watch and guard, against the enemy that led out from God, out of life and truth. For all the sufferings are by and through him that is out of the truth.

50 All have been plunged into sin and death from the life, for... they have been all subjected by the evil spirit, which hath led them out of the truth into the evil.

51 By this invisible spirit I discerned all the false hearing, the false seeing, and the false smelling, which was above the spirit, quenching and grieving it; and that all that were there were in confusion and deceit.

52 Now will I arise, saith the Lord God Almighty, to trample and thunder down deceit, which hath long reigned and stained the earth.

before the Lord you hypocrites, pay attention to the light of God in you which shows you the deceit in your hearts, and obey the light.

46 The devil didn't stay with the truth. So when the Jews abandoned the truth it was said they were 'of the devil'.... And there is no promise from God to the devil that he shall one day return to the truth again. But there is a promise from God to the man and woman who were deceived by the devil (Genesis 3).... And much more of all this was opened up to me, but it is too big for me to speak about.

47 The Ranters argued that God made the devil, but I denied this and explained to them that... he became the devil by leaving the truth and thus becoming a murderer and destroyer. So I demonstrated that God did not make the devil since God is a God of truth and made all things good and blessed them.

48 The snake... that led the man away from God, he is the prince of the world, the prince of darkness, and... the father of lies, a murderer from the beginning, the corrupter of humankind, the one who originally brought about sin and the separation from God.

49 Each one of you stay awake and on your guard against the enemy that led [us] away from God, away from life and truth. For all [our] suffering comes as a result of his departing from truth.

50 Everyone has plunged from life into sin and death, for... they have all been brought under the power of the evil spirit which led them away from truth and into evil.

51 With the help of this invisible spirit I was able to discern all the false hearing, the false seeing and the false smelling which were prevailing over this spirit, stifling and grieving it. And I could see that everyone there was in confusion and in deceit.

52 Now will I arise, says the Lord God Almighty, to trample and thunder down deceit, which for too long has ruled and damaged the earth.

THE VEILED MIND

53 Dwell in that which is pure of God in you, lest your thoughts get forth; and then evil thoughts get up, and surmising one against another, which ariseth out of the veiled mind, which darkens the pure discerning.

54 Though you see little, and know little, and have little, and see your emptiness, and see your nakedness, and barrenness, and unfruitfulness, and see the hardness of your hearts, and your own unworthiness; it is the light that discovers all this, and the love of God to you, and it is that which is immediate, but the dark understanding cannot comprehend it.... When your minds run into any thing outwardly, without the power, it covers and veils the pure in you.

55 Heed not the eyes of the world, ye prophets of the Lord, but answer that in them all which they have closed their eye to.

56 Give not way to the lazy, dreaming mind, for it enters into the temptations.

TURNING

57 Inspiration and revelation, while their minds are erred from the spirit of God in themselves, are hid from them. So when their minds are turned with the light and spirit of God, towards God, then with it they shall know something of revelation and inspiration; as they are turned with that of God from the evil, and emptied of that, then there will be some room in them for something of God to be revealed and inspired into them.

58 Mind the light of God in your consciences, which will show you all deceit; dwelling in it, guides out of the many things into one spirit, which cannot lie, nor deceive.... Dis-

THE VEILED MIND

53 Focus on that divine part of you which is pure, otherwise your thoughts wander off and other, bad thoughts arise, one contradicting or condemning another, and all this arises from the veiled mind which darkens any pure discernment [of what is happening].

54 Although you may see only a little and know little and have little, and although you see your nakedness and futility and uselessness, and see the hardness of your hearts and your own unworthiness, it is the light that reveals all this to you, and the love of God for you. It is also something [in you] which is quite immediate, but the dark mind cannot grasp it.... When your minds get taken up with something external, without reference to the power [within you], it covers and veils what is pure in you.

55 Don't pay attention to the eyes of the world, you prophets of the Lord, but reflect back what it is in them they have closed their eye to.

56 Don't give way to the lazy, dreaming mind, for then you've as good as given in to temptation.

TURNING

57 Inspiration and revelation are hidden from them as long as their minds stray from the spirit of God within them. So when, with the help of the light and the spirit of God, their minds are turned towards God then they shall know something of revelation and inspiration. As they are turned away from the cause of trouble [within them] and emptied of it, some space will be made for something of God to be revealed and inspired in them.

58 Pay attention to the light of God in your conscience and it will show up deceit wherever it appears. Focusing on that leads you out of an

cover all deceit, and rend all veils and coverings, that the
pure may come to life, which deceit hath trampled upon.

59 All friends of the Lord every where, whose minds are
turned within towards the Lord, take heed and hearken to
the light within you, which is the light of Christ and of
God, which will call your minds to within (as ye heed it),
which were abroad in the creatures; that by it your minds
may be renewed, and by it turned to God.... And the light
of God, that calls your minds out of the creatures, turns
them to God, to an endless being, joy and peace.

SILENCE

60 Mark and consider in silence, in lowliness of mind, and
thou wilt hear the Lord speak unto thee in thy mind.

61 Be still and cool in thy own mind and spirit from thy own
thoughts, and then thou wilt feel the principle of God to
turn thy mind to the Lord God, whereby thou wilt receive
his strength and power from whence life comes, to allay all
tempests, against blusterings and storms.... Therefore be
still a while from thy own thoughts, searching, seeking,
desires and imaginations, and be stayed in the principle of
God in thee, to stay thy mind upon God, up to God; and
thou wilt find strength from him and find him to be a
present help in time of trouble, in need, and to be a God at
hand.

62 Be still and silent from thy own wisdom, wit, craft, subtilty
or policy that would arise in thee, but stand single to the
Lord, without any end to thyself.

63 But all you that be in your own wisdom and in your own
reason, you tell that silent waiting upon God is famine to
you; it is a strange life to you to come to be silent, you must
come into a new world. Now you must die in the silence,

obsession with many 'things' into a sense of the one spirit, which is incapable of lying or deceiving [you].... Unmask all deceit and tear away all veils and coverings so that the pure, which has been suppressed by deceit, may then come to life.

59 All friends of the Lord everywhere, who have turned inwardly towards the Lord, be alert and listen to the light inside you. This is the light of Christ and of God, and, as you listen to it, it will call you inside, whereas previously you were taken up with things out there, and it will renew you spiritually and turn you to God.... And the light, that calls you away from a preoccupation with things, turns you to God, and to an endless being, joy and peace.

SILENCE

60 Listen and consider in silence, in an attitude of humility, and you will hear the Lord speak to you in your mind.

61 Be still and cool in your own mind and spirit, free from your own thoughts, and you will then feel the divine source of life in you turn your mind to the Lord God. And in doing this you will receive his strength and life-giving power to quieten every storm and gale that blows against you.... Therefore be still for a while from your own thoughts, your own searching, seeking, desiring, imagining, and rest on the divine source of life within you so as to rest your mind on God himself and to come close to God. You will then find strength from him and find him to be a present help in time of trouble, in time of need, and to be a God at hand.

62 Be still and silent in your mind, giving up any wise, clever or subtle thoughts of your own that may arise in your mind, and be open and honest to the Lord, without any thought of what you yourself may get out of it.

63 But all you who rely on your own wisdom and your own reason, you make out that silent waiting on God would leave you famished. It

die from the wisdom, die from the knowledge, die from the
reason, and die from the understanding.

64 Wait in the life, which will keep you above words.

65 So here every spirit comes to have a particular satisfaction
and quietness in his own mind, and here the weary come
to have rest in Christ.... Such shall find mercy of God
when their minds are guided up unto God and their spirits
and minds are quieted in silent waiting upon God. In one half
hour they have more peace and satisfaction than they have
had from all other teachers of the world all their lifetime.

66 We came through that country into Cumberland again
where we had a general meeting of many thousands of
people atop of a hill, near Langlands. Heavenly and glorious it was and the glory of the Lord did shine over all, and
there were as many as one could well speak over, there was
such a multitude. Their eyes were kept to Christ their
teacher and they came to sit under their vine, and afterwards a Friend in the ministry, Francis Howgill, went
amongst them, and when he was moved to stand up
amongst them he saw they had no need of words for they
were all sitting down under their teacher Christ Jesus; so he
was moved to sit down again amongst them without speaking anything.

67 Much more might I write concerning these things but they
are hard to be uttered, or to be borne; for there has so much
strife and foolishness entered the minds of people, and a
want of the stillness and quietness in the pure spirit of God,
in which things are revealed that have been veiled; in which
things are opened that have been hid, and uncovered that
have been covered.

would indeed be a strange life to you to learn to be silent; you would have to enter a new world. Now you have to die in the silence, you with your wisdom, your knowledge, your reason and your own understanding.

64 Stay with the experience of the life [within you], and this will free you from a dependence on words.

65 So here every person comes to find a particular satisfaction and quietness in his or her own mind, and those who are weary can relax in Christ.... If their minds are guided towards God and if their minds and spirits are calmed in silent waiting on God, then they find mercy from God. In one half hour they gain more peace and satisfaction than they have known from all other teachers of the world the whole of their lifetime.

66 We travelled through that country into Cumberland again, where we had a general meeting of many thousands of people on top of a hill near Langlands. Heavenly and glorious it was, and the glory of the Lord shone over everyone. And there were so many people there I would hardly have been able to make myself heard. Yet their eyes were fixed on their teacher Christ and they all 'sat under their vine'. And later a Friend in the ministry, Francis Howgill, joined them, and when he was moved to stand up among them he saw they had no need of words because they were sitting at the feet of their teacher Christ Jesus. So he was moved to sit down among them again without saying anything.

67 I could write much more about these things, but they are hard to express, and also hard to take, because people now have so much conflict and foolishness in their minds that they fail to experience the quiet and stillness in the pure spirit of God where things are revealed that have been veiled, where things are opened up that have been hidden, and where things are uncovered that have been covered up.

THE LIGHT

68 The light is that by which ye come to see.

69 Now this is the light which you are lighted withal, which shows you when you do wrong...; and you know with that when you have wronged anyone, and broken promise, and told a thing that is not so, there is something riseth in you that is a witness against you, and that is the light.

70 That which may be known of God is made manifest within you, which God hath showed you, that when you do the thing which is not convenient, not righteous, but worthy of death, by that of God in you you can tell.

71 There was a doctor that did dispute with us, which was of great service and occasion of opening much to the people concerning the light and the spirit. And he so opposed it in everyone, that I called an Indian because he denied it to be in them, and I asked him if that he did lie and do that to another which he would not have them do the same to him, and when he did wrong was not there something in him, that did tell him of it, that he should not do so, but did reprove him. And he said there was such a thing in him.

72 If all men would come to the knowledge of the truth they must come to that which doth reprove them, and lead them into all truth.

73 The light is that which exercises the conscience towards God, and towards man, where it is loved.

74 As the light opens and exercises thy conscience, it will... let thee see invisible things, which are clearly seen by that which is invisible in thee.... That which is invisible is the light within thee, which he who is invisible has given thee a measure of. That will let thee see thy heart.

THE LIGHT

68 The light is what enables you to see.

69 Now this is the light that enlightens you: it shows you when you do wrong.... And you know that when you have wronged someone or broken a promise or said something that isn't true, there is something that rises up within you to bear witness against you. And that is the light.

70 What may be known of God is disclosed within you. God himself has made you aware of it. It is this: when you do something that is not appropriate, not right, something that should never have happened, you know all this yourself because of that something of God in you.

71 There was a certain doctor who disagreed with us, but it proved to be a great opportunity for helping the people understand the light and the spirit. He denied that the light existed in everyone, especially in the Indians, so I called an Indian and asked him if, when he lied or did to someone else what he wouldn't accept from them or did any wrong, there was something in him that told him this, something that told him that he should not do these things, and told him off for doing them. And he said there was such a thing in him.

72 If people want to know the truth they must first accept what it is that reproves them, for that is what will lead them to all the truth.

73 The light is what activates the conscience towards God and towards fellow human beings, so long as it is loved.

74 As the light illuminates and activates your conscience it will... let you see things that can't be seen [by the physical eye], but can be seen by the invisible [eye] within you.... And this invisible [source of seeing] is the light inside you, which you have been given a portion of

75 But oh, then did I see my troubles, trials, and temptations more than ever I had done! As the light appeared, all appeared that is out of the light, darkness, death, temptations, the unrighteous, the ungodly; all was manifest and seen in the light.... And then the spiritual discerning came into me, by which I did discern my own thoughts, groans and sighs, and what it was that did veil me, and what it was that did open me.

76 If you love this light it will teach you, walking up and down and lying in bed, and never let you speak a vain word.

77 Now the Lord God hath opened to me by his invisible power how that every man was enlightened by the divine light of Christ; and I saw it shine through all, and that they that believed in it came out of condemnation and came to the light of life and became children of it.... This I saw in the pure openings of the light without the help of any man, neither did I then know where to find it in the scriptures; though afterwards, searching the scriptures, I found it.

78 As I was walking I heard old people and workpeople to say, 'He is such a man as never was, he knows people's thoughts', for I turned them to the divine light of Christ and his spirit that let them see all their thoughts, words, and actions.

79 'The path of the just is a shining light', the path of the unjust is darkness. So there are but two paths. Now the unjust cannot abide to hear talk of the light, but call it natural, and created and made, or conscience, they do not know what to call it, whose darkness cannot comprehend the light, though it shines in the darkness.

80 So then I took a Bible and let them see that the made and created, natural lights were the sun, moon and stars, and the

by the one who is himself invisible. This will let you see your heart.

75 But oh dear, that's when I saw my troubles and tribulations more than
I have ever done before! As the light appeared everything that was out
of the light also appeared: darkness, death, temptations, whatever was
not right or good. Everything was disclosed and seen in the light.…
And then I received a spiritual discernment which enabled me to
discern my own thoughts, longings and desires, and to see what it was
that obscured my vision and what it was that opened it up.

76 If you love this light it will teach you, whether you are up and about
or lying in bed, and it will never let you say what you don't really
mean.

77 Now the Lord God opened me up by a power I couldn't [physically]
see, and made me aware that everyone was enlightened by the divine
light of Christ. I saw it shine through everyone. And I saw that those
who believed in it came out of their guilt and shame, and came into
the light of life and became children of light.… I saw all this as the
light itself opened it up to me, and without any human help. Nor did
I then know where to find it in the scriptures, though later, looking
through the scriptures, I did find it.

78 As I was walking along I heard some old people and workers say, 'He's
like nobody who ever lived. He knows what people are thinking!'
They said this because I had turned their attention to the divine light
of Christ and his spirit which then made them aware of their every
thought, word and action.

79 'The path of the just is a shining light', the path of the unjust is darkness. So there are only two paths. Now the unjust can't abide hearing
talk of the light. They call it 'natural' and 'created' and 'made', or 'conscience' – they do not know what to call it. The darkness in them
simply cannot grasp what the light is, even though it is shining in the
darkness.

elements; but the true light which John bore witness to was the life in Christ the Word, by which all things were made and created. And it was called the light in man and woman, which was the true light which had enlightened every man that came into the world, which was a heavenly and divine light.

SELF-AWARENESS

81 For with the light man sees himself.

82 Therefore all now awake from sleep and see where you are. Let the light of Jesus Christ, that shines in everyone of your consciences, search you thoroughly, and it will let you clearly see.

83 Mind the pure light of God in you, which shows your sin and evil, and how you have spent your time; and shows you how your minds go forth.

84 Neither lay open one another's weaknesses behind one another's backs.... But every one of you in particular with the light of Christ (which he hath enlightened you withal) see yourselves, that self may be judged out with the light in everyone. Now, all loving the light here no self can stand, but it is judged with the light; and here all are in unity, and here no self-will can arise, no mastery; but all that is judged out.

85 Which light being owned, self, and the righteousness of self, come to be denied.

86 Walk in the truth... stand all naked, bare and uncovered before the Lord.

87 If ye love the light it will let you see all your evil thoughts, words and actions, which be wrought out of God, and turn you from them; and coming into the light your works will

80 So then I took a Bible and let them see that the lights that were 'made, created, natural' were the sun, moon and stars, and the elements. But the true light John bore witness to was 'the life' in Christ, 'the word' by which everything had been created and made. And it was also called 'the light' in men and women because it was the 'true light which enlightens everyone who comes into the world'. So it was a transcendent and divine light.

SELF-AWARENESS

81 For with the light you see yourself.

82 Now therefore all of you wake up from your sleep and see where you are. Let the light of Jesus Christ, that shines in the conscience of every one of you, search you thoroughly. It will then let you see clearly.

83 Pay attention to the pure light of God in you. It is this that makes you aware of what you have done wrong, how you have [mis]spent your time, and how your minds have projected [on to things outside].

84 Also, don't expose one another's weaknesses behind one another's backs…. Instead, let every one of you individually, with the help of the light that Christ has enlightened you with, look at yourselves, so that self, the ego, might be excluded by the light in each one of you. Then, with each of you loving the light, no ego can stand up, because the light exposes it. And in this situation you all have unity, and no self-assertion can arise, no desire to control, because all this is exposed.

85 Accepting the light, you find you can no longer accept the ego with its pretension to being always right.

86 Live your life in the truth… being open, naked, exposed before the Lord.

87 If you love the light it will let you see all the bad things you have

be wrought in God, and your words will be from him, and
so good.

88 Therefore to the light I direct you, that with it ye may see
yourselves; then in it stand, that with it ye may see Jesus,
from whence it comes.

THE WAY TO PEACE

89 In that light that shows you all this, stand, neither go to
the right hand nor to the left; here patience is exercised,
here is thy will subjected, here thou wilt see the mercies of
God made manifest in death.... For the first step to peace
is to stand still in the light (which discovers things contrary to it) for power and strength to stand against that
nature which the light discovers: for here grace grows, here
is God alone glorified and exalted, and the unknown truth,
unknown to the world, made manifest.

90 Whatever ye are addicted to, the tempter will come in that
thing; and when he can trouble you, then he gets advantage over you, and then ye are gone. Stand still in that
which is pure, after ye see yourselves; and then mercy
comes in. After thou seest thy thoughts, and the temptations, do not think, but submit; and then power comes.
Stand still in that which shows and discovers; and there
doth strength immediately come. And stand still in the
light, submit to it, and the other will be hushed and gone;
and then content comes.... Your strength is to stand still,
after ye see yourselves.

91 This is the word of the Lord God unto you all: what the light
doth make manifest and discover, temptations, confusions,
distractions, distempers; do not look at the temptations,
confusions, corruptions, but at the light that discovers
them, that makes them manifest; and with the same light
you will feel over them, to receive power to stand against

thought, said and done – bad because God had no part in them – and
it will turn you away from those things. And as you come into the light
you will find that God is involved in what you do, and that what you
say will come from him and therefore be good.

88 So, I'm pointing you to the light so that you will see yourselves.
Then stand there, in the light, so that you will also see Jesus from
whom the light comes.

THE WAY TO PEACE

89 When you see all this in the light stand still. Don't turn away to the
left or the right. This is where you will need to be patient, where your
ego will be brought down, where, in what seems like death to you,
you will experience the forgiveness of God.… For the first step to
peace is to stand still in the light – the light that reveals whatever is
opposed to it. And standing still there you will receive the power and
strength to resist that part of you which the light has exposed. Because
this is where grace grows, where God alone is seen to be glorious and
powerful, and where the unknown truth – unknown to the world out
there – is revealed.

90 Whatever it is you are addicted to that's where the tempter will get
you. If he can trouble you there he gets an advantage over you, and
then you are finished. So see what's happening to you, what you are
doing, then wait there in the light of what is pure in you, and you
will find forgiveness. When you have seen what's going on in your
mind, and the temptations there, do not think, just submit [to reality].
You will then receive power. If you stand still in that [light] that
exposes and reveals, you will find that strength is immediately given to
you. So, stand still in the light, submit to it, and all the rest will quieten
down or disappear. You will then be contented.… Your strength is to
stand still, once you have seen yourselves.

91 This is what the Lord God has to say to you all: when the light discloses and reveals things to you, things that tempt you, confuse you,
distract you and the like, don't go on looking at them, but look at the

them.... For looking down at sin, and corruption, and distraction, you are swallowed up in it; but looking at the light that discovers them, you will see over them. That will give victory; and you will find grace and strength; and there is the first step to peace.

THE OPENING OF THE EYE

92 So God Almighty open your understandings, all people everywhere, that you may see yourselves. And if you take heed to that light which will exercise your consciences, it will let you see yourselves, which eye is the light, and this light will let you see God; but if your minds go forth, the god of this world cometh in and takes the dominion, and so your minds are blinded and your understandings darkened.... Lay aside all contention and striving about words, which is no profit, but mind the pure light of God within, which will teach everyone to know God.

93 Dwell in that which is pure, that ye may be able to discern, and savour, and comprehend that which is not pure; and wait in that which is pure, to have your minds guided
94 thereby, which will let you see God. ... For God is not seen but in the eternal light whence all pure wisdom comes. This treasure is not seen but with the spiritual eye; nor received but with the pure in heart, and by those who dwell and abide in the eternal light.

95 Ye... are led by the witness of God up to God. And such as go from it, upon them the law of God is to be added, and they by it to be stopped and limited; which law is a praise to them that do well.... And in this that eye is opened which beholds God and his law, which answers that of God in everyone.

96 All to live in that which is the same today, as was yesterday... so, no new thing, but that which was and is to all eternity;

light that has made you aware of them. And with this same light you will feel yourself rising above them and empowered to resist them.... For so long as you keep looking down at what is basically wrong – your being corrupted, distracted, or whatever – you are dragged down into it. But looking at the light that discloses them you can see over the top of them, and that enables you to overcome them, and you will find grace and strength. And there is the first step to peace.

THE OPENING OF THE EYE

92 So may God Almighty open the minds of every one of you, everywhere, so that you can see yourselves. And if you pay attention to that light in you that activates your conscience, it will enable you to see yourselves. And this eye in you, the light, will enable you to see God. But if your mind becomes preoccupied [with things] 'the god of this world' gets into it and takes over (2 Corinthians 4:4), then your mind is blinded and your understanding is dimmed.... Lay aside all arguments about words, which are of no profit to anyone, and give your attention to the pure light of God inside you. This will teach everyone to know God.

93 Live with what is pure, and you will then be able to discern and savour and grasp what is not pure. Stay with what is pure, to allow your minds to be guided by it, and it will let you see God.

94 For God can only be seen in the eternal light from which all pure wisdom derives. This treasure can only be seen with the spiritual eye; it can only be received by those who are pure in heart, those who live and remain in the eternal light.

95 It is the witness of God [in you] that brings you close to God. But some people ignore it, so in addition they get the law of God, which is intended to stop them and limit them, though it does credit to those who do what it says.... And with this [witness in you] an eye is opened that can recognise God and his law, because the law reflects that something of God in everyone.

let your fellowship be in that, and your unity and commu-
nion be in that; for by the spiritual eye the eternal unity with
the eternal God is seen. So, hear his voice everywhere.

97 So eye the Lord God in all things in the spirit, who is a
spirit; in that ye may distinguish his things, and the things
that are of your selves, and what is of men, and what is of
God, and what to keep alive, and what must die. So be obedient to the spirit, and to the good power of God, that hath
quickened you; and live in it, that ye may die no more, for
that gives you life.

98 Live in the light, which was before darkness was, and the
power of it; in which light is also your everlasting fellowship; and in this you will know God's dwelling, which is in
the light.

THE CHRIST WITHIN

99 We say, that the word of God is the original, which
doth fulfil the scriptures; and the word is it which
makes a divine, which is called a hammer, but it is a living
hammer; and is called a sword and fire, but it is a living
sword, and a living fire, to hammer, and cut down, and
burn up that which separated and kept man from God; by
which word man is reconciled again to God, which is called
the word of reconciliation; by this word are men and
women sanctified and made clean. And this is the word that
makes both men and women divine, and brings them into
the divine nature, which hammers and cuts down that
which corrupted their nature; and by this word are they
brought into a divine wisdom, understanding, knowledge,
spirit and power.... And by this word they do see all flesh
to be as grass, and as the flower of the field that fadeth; and
the word of God that lives, and abides and endures for ever
is Christ, whose name is called the Word of God.

96 All of you live in that reality that is the same today as it was yesterday… so nothing new, only what has been and will be to all eternity. Let that be the source of your fellowship together, and of your unity and community. For with the spiritual eye you can see the eternal unity with the eternal God. So hear his voice everywhere.

97 So eye the Lord God in everything – in the spirit, because he is a spirit. In doing this you will be able to distinguish between what is his and what is yours, what comes from God and what comes from humans, and what to keep alive and what to leave to die. So be obedient to the spirit and to the good power of God which brought you to life. And live by that power so that you may never die again – for that is what gives you life.

98 Live in the light which existed before darkness ever came about, before it ever acquired its power. In this light you also experience a fellowship that lasts forever (1 John 1:7), and in this light you will come to know where God dwells, because that too is in the light (1 Timothy 6:16).

THE CHRIST WITHIN

99 We claim that the first word to be spoken, the word from which all other words are derived, is the word spoken by God. This word makes sense of the scriptures, it makes someone capable of speaking about God. It is called 'a hammer', but it is a living hammer, and it is called 'a sword' and 'a fire', but it is a living sword and a living fire, because it is meant to hammer and cut down and burn up whatever separated people from God and kept them away from him. So by this word people are reconciled to God again, which is why it is called 'the word of reconciliation'. And by this word men and women are made holy and clean. And this is the word that makes both men and women divine and brings them into the divine nature, the word which hammers and cuts down what corrupted their nature. And by this word they are brought into a divine wisdom, understanding, knowledge, spirit and power.… And by this word they can see that 'all mortals are like grass… like the flower of the field… [that] fades; but

100 Many of the people stayed and I turned them to the light of Christ by which they might see their sins and see their saviour Christ Jesus, who was their way to God and their mediator that made their peace betwixt them and God.

101 Keep within. And when they shall say, 'lo here', or 'lo there is Christ', go not forth; for Christ is within you. And they are seducers and antichrists, which draw your minds out from the teaching within you.

102 He that feeleth the light that Christ hath enlightened him withal, he feeleth Christ in his mind, which is the power of the cross of Christ, and shall not need to have a cross of wood or stone to put him in the mind of Christ or his cross, which is the power of God.

103 And know you not yourselves how that Christ is in you, except you be reprobates; and if he be witnessed within and known within then he is come, then what need you have bread and wine to put you in remembrance of him?

104 If thou hadst lived at that day (thou mayst say), thou wouldst not have put Christ to death. But thou shalt see the same nature in thee now, as was then. For now is the son of God come; and ye are of the same generation that they were.

THE SEED

105 I saw the harvest white, and the seed of God lying thick in the ground, as ever did wheat that was sown outwardly, and none to gather it; for this I mourned with tears.... This was the earth in people's hearts, which was to be shaken before the seed of God was raised out of the earth. And it was so; for the Lord's power began to shake them, and great meetings we began to have, and a mighty power and work of God there was amongst people, to the astonishment of both people and priests.

the word of the Lord endures for evermore' (1 Peter 1:24f) and that
that word is Christ, whose name is 'the Word of God'.

100 Many of the people stayed and I turned their attention to the light
of Christ which would enable them to see both what they were doing
wrong and who could save them from all that, Christ Jesus. He was
their way to God and their mediator who would make peace between
them and God.

101 Stay inside. And when they say 'Look here', or 'Look, there is Christ',
don't go out there, for Christ is inside you. And those who try to
seduce you and draw your minds away from the teaching inside you
are opposed to Christ.

102 Whoever feels the light that Christ has enlightened them with feels
Christ himself in their mind. And since this [experience] is what makes
the cross of Christ powerful, they won't need a cross of wood or stone
to remind them of Christ or his cross, which is 'the power of God' (1
Corinthians 1:23f).

103 Surely you realise that Christ is in you. If not then you have fallen
away. But if you do, and have seen him for yourselves and known him
within, then he has come. And what need then for bread and wine to
remind you of him?

104 If you had lived at that time, you may say, you would not have put
Christ to death. But you will find the same disposition in you now as
they had then. For the son of God has come now, and you are of the
same generation as they were.

THE SEED

105 I saw the harvest all white, and the seed of God lying thick on the
ground, as real as any wheat that had been sown physically, and no one
to gather it. For this I mourned with tears.... This was the earth in
people's hearts which had to be broken up before the seed of God
could be raised out of the earth. And so it was, for the Lord's power
began to break them up. And great meetings we began to have, and

106 Hearken to the light within thee, and it will let thee see the
    secret places...; and as a prison without thee, so there is a
    prison within, where the seed of God lies; and as there is a
    threshing without thee, it will let thee see threshing within
    thee; chaff without thee, the chaff within...; for man being
    drove into the earth, and the earth being above the seed; so
    as the earth without thee, so the earth within thee... com-
    parisons like to that nature in man; that man may look
    upon the creation with that which is invisible, and there
    read himself.

107 For the Lord hath a seed that ways, if ye in patience all of
    you wait, and not matter the weather, the storms, the
    winds, the hail, the rain, when ye are to sow the seed, nor
    the rough ground that is to be tilled. For the husbandman
    waits patiently after the seed is sown; there is a winter
    before the summer comes. And there must be a great work
    before the misty heathen be cleared in their understandings
    (that are so naturally) and the dark air be driven back, and
    the prince of life and light be witnessed.

108 So, in the seed of God live, and lie down in the same, which
    is Christ, the life, the way to God the Father of life.

109 There is... no true seed, but what Christ hath sown in the
    heart.

110 Keep your meetings, and ye will feel the seed of God among
    you all, though never a word be spoken among you.

FEELING

111 Be faithful unto the Lord God, minding the seed, and
    feeling it and knowing it in yourselves.

112 And feel the seed of God over all that which makes to
    suffer, and it will remain when all that is gone, in that ye
    will feel life over death, and light over darkness.

there was a mighty power and work of God among people, to the astonishment of both people and priests.

106 Listen to the light inside you and it will let you see the secret places.... And as there is a prison outside you, so there is a prison inside, where the seed of God lies. And as there is threshing outside you, [the light] will let you see threshing inside you, chaff outside you, the chaff inside.... And since humans have been driven into the earth, so that there is earth above the seed, there is earth inside you, just as there is earth outside you... comparisons in nature to what happens in humans, so that humans may look on the creation with what itself cannot be seen, and there read themselves.

107 For the Lord has a seed out there, if only you all had the patience to wait, and not bother about the weather when the time comes for sowing the seed – the storms, the winds, the hail, the rain – or the roughness of the ground which has to be tilled. For the farmer waits patiently once the seed is sown: there's a winter to be got through before the summer comes. And there's a great work to be done before the mists can be cleared that befog people's minds – which is natural enough – and the dark air blown away so that people at last can see the prince of life and light.

108 So live on the seed, lie down in it; this is Christ, the life, the way to God the father of life.

109 The only real seed is the seed that Christ has sown in the heart.

110 Maintain your meetings and you will feel the seed of God among you all, even though nothing is said between you.

FEELING

111 Be faithful to the Lord God, attending to the seed, feeling it and being aware of it in yourselves.

112 And feel the seed of God rise powerfully above whatever makes you suffer, and it will remain there when all the suffering is gone because

113 Keep in the truth that ye may see and feel the Lord's presence amongst you.

114 And all Friends, live in the power of the Lord God and keep down the wise part, which will judge truth to be simple and come to despise it, and cry up their own words of wisdom in its place.

115 Keep in the power of the Lord God.... There is the wisdom which is pure.... Feel it in the heart, which is more than in the head or tongue, which many may strive for, but do not obtain.... Therefore all be wise in the wisdom of God.... In that ye will feel his presence and blessing.

116 'For with the heart man doth believe, and with the mouth confession is made unto salvation.' First, he has it in his heart before it comes out of his mouth, and this is beyond that brain-beaten-heady stuff which man has long studied about the saints' words.

117 All ye that have felt the light and have been turned to it, in that light ye feel the covenant with God, who is light, which brings to be acquainted with the life of God.

118 All people that are gone from the witness of God in their own particulars, they are all weak and feeble and staggering: all men's and women's strength is in the power of God which goes over the power of darkness. So, feel all this in you, to carry you through all and over all, and in it preach and work for God, and let your ear be lent to it, and hearken to it in one another, and by it feel the seed raised up in one another.

119 Therefore every one receive Christ the light that hath enlightened you, and ye shall feel the power.

you will experience life as stronger than death, and light as stronger than darkness.

113 Stay with the truth so that you may see and feel the Lord's presence among you.

114 Friends, all of you, live by the power of the Lord God and hold down that part of you which thinks it is wise, which thinks truth is 'simple' and so comes to despise it, preferring instead its own words of wisdom.

115 Stay in the power of the Lord God.... That's where you'll find a pure wisdom.... Feel it in the heart, which is more than you ever find in the head or hear spoken, and which many strive for but fail to obtain.... Therefore be wise, all of you, in the wisdom of God.... Then you will feel his presence and blessing.

116 'For faith comes from the heart, and the confession that leads to salvation comes from the lips' (Romans 10:10). First of all it is in the heart, before it comes out of the mouth, and that is beyond all that brain-bashing, heady stuff that people have mostly got into when they study the words of the saints [who wrote the Bible].

117 What you are experiencing, those of you who have felt the light and turned to it, is 'the covenant of light' (Isaiah 42:6), that is, a relationship which God himself has established – since God is light – to make it possible for us to know God's life for ourselves.

118 Everyone who has turned away from God's witness in their own personal experience has become weak and feeble and insecure: the strength of every man and woman lies in the power of God which overrides the power of darkness. So feel all this in you, and it will carry you through and over everything [that threatens you]. Speak to people about it, do your work for God in it, bend your ear to it, listen to it in one another, and with its help feel the seed growing in one another.

119 Therefore everyone, welcome Christ the light who has enlightened you and you will feel the power.

LIFE

120 He that loves the light, and walks in the light, receives the light of life.

121 Through the light that enlighteneth them they have life... they have salvation, they have truth, they have peace with God.

122 That which calls your minds out of the earth, turns them towards God, where the pure babe is born in the virgin mind.

123 Therefore be rich in life and in grace which will endure, ye who are heirs of life, and born of the womb of eternity.

124 Heed everywhere the life of God, and do not gad abroad from the truth within.... And so, having your food within, ye shall not go forth to gather it.

125 Keep your habitations, that ye may every one feel your spring in the light which comes from the Lord, and feel your nourishment and refreshment; which waters the plants and causeth them to grow up in the Lord, from whom the pure, living springs come.

HEALING

126 Feel all of you the power of the Lord God in yourselves to guide your minds up to God, and to give you dominion over all weakness, and to strengthen and to heal you.

127 Now as the principle of God in thee hath been transgressed, come to it, to keep thy mind down low, up to the Lord God; and deny thyself. And from thy own will, that is, the earthly, thou must be kept. Then thou wilt feel the power of God that will bring nature into his course, and to see the glory of the first body. And there the wisdom of God will be received, which is Christ, by which all things

LIFE

120 Anyone who loves the light and lives in the light receives the light of life.

121 Through the light that enlightens them they have life… they have salvation, they have truth, they have peace with God.

122 What calls you away from material things also turns you towards God, where a pure baby is born in your virgin mind.

123 Therefore be rich in life and in grace that will last, you heirs of life, born of the womb of eternity.

124 Be aware of the life of God wherever you are, and don't wander off from the truth inside you…. So, having your food inside, you won't need to go out to fetch it.

125 Look after the place you live in, so that you each become aware of the spring of water emerging in the light from the Lord, and aware of the source of your nourishment and refreshment. It is this that waters the plants and makes them grow in the Lord, from whom indeed these pure springs of life all come.

HEALING

126 If you can all feel the power of the Lord God within you, it will lead you closer to God, enable you to overcome all weakness, and strengthen and heal you.

127 Now since the divine source of light in you has been opposed, you have to come back to it to gain an attitude of humility towards God, and you have to reject the claims of your 'self'. You must be kept from asserting your own will, that is, the merely human part of you, then you will feel the power of God that will set nature on its course, and you will experience the glory of the body as it was meant to be. And

were made and created, in wisdom to be preserved and ordered to God's glory. There thou wilt come to receive and feel the physician of value, which clothes people in their right mind.

THE PROCESS

128   All you who love the light, you love God and Christ, and if you love it and obey it, it will lead you out of darkness, out of your evil deeds into the light of life, into the way of peace and into the life and power of truth.

129   Let not any of you in your desires wander from that which is pure in you; then your conditions will be kept clear and pure to see all things as they are, and a clear separation will be made from that which is of man, and of your own, and that which is of God; and there will be a growing up in that which is pure.

130   So wait all in the power of the Lord, and in the light, in which you will feel life and peace and the Lord's blessing.... And in peace and love live, in the spirit and power of God, in which is the unity and the fellowship in the bond of peace, that truth and life may reign amongst you; that in all things you may adorn and grace the truth, that never hath an end.

131   Therefore live in the truth, which the devil is out of, and in the life, which was before death... and in the light, which was before darkness... and in this ye will have fellowship with God, with Christ and one with another. And so no more, but my love.

in this process you will receive the wisdom of God by which everything was made and created – that is Christ (1 Corinthians 1:23,24) – so that everything may be preserved and ordered with wisdom, to realise God's glory. In all this you will come to experience and feel 'the physician of value' (Job 13:4) who clothes people in their right mind.

THE PROCESS

128 Everyone of you who loves the light, you are loving God and Christ as well. And if you go on loving it and obeying it, it will lead you out of darkness and out of your wrongdoing, into the light of life, into the way of peace and into the life and power of truth.

129 Let none of you, out of desire, wander from that part of you which is pure. You will then have the clarity and purity of mind to see things as they are. You will be able to distinguish clearly between what is human – and therefore your own – and what is divine. And you will find yourselves growing in that state of purity.

130 So if you all wait in the power of the Lord and in the light, you will experience life and peace and the Lord's blessing.... And if you live in peace and love, in the spirit and power of God, you will have unity in these things and fellowship in the bond of peace. In this way truth and life will be able to rule among you, and in everything you do you will be able to adorn and honour the truth that lasts forever.

131 Therefore live with reality, which the devil has abandoned. Live in this life that existed before death ever happened.... And live in the light which existed before darkness appeared.... In doing this you will have fellowship with God, with Christ, and with one another. So no more now from me, but my love.

ENDNOTES for part one

1. A paper of 1652, in *The journal of George Fox* (hereafter *Journal*), ed. Thomas Ellwood, in *The works of George Fox*, vols. 1 and 2 (hereafter *Works*), Philadelphia, 1831 (reprinted by New Foundation, 1990), vol. 1, pp.166f; in *Works* 1:166f. Cf. *Journal*, ed. John Nickalls, Cambridge University Press, 1952, pp.142f. 'Idols' temples' is Fox's phrase for churches, in the sense of buildings, but 'the church', for him, was the gathered people of God; see Glossary on 'steeple house' and extracts 1:3,23; 2:9,10.

2. A paper of 1656, in *Journal*, ed. Ellwood, in *Works* 1:304.

3. 'To all who love the Lord Jesus Christ' (1654), in the collection of papers and tracts known as *The Gospel Truth demonstrated in a collection of doctrinal books* (hereafter *Doctrinals*) in *Works* 4:47. Cf. Acts 2:47 for 'his church'; for the rest Ecclesiastes 12:3, Isaiah 2:17-21.

4. Manuscript Item 104.E (no date), bound with the Annual Catalogue, in Friends House Library, London, quoted in Hugh McGregor Ross, ed., *George Fox speaks for himself*, Sessions, York, 1991, pp.25f; cf pp.135,140 for details of the Annual Catalogue, published in 1669, and the manuscript papers bound with it. 'God... forbids you to make an image' probably refers to the second of the ten commandments: Exodus 20:4-6. For the rest cf. Isaiah 40:12-25; Romans 1:19-23.

5. Epistle 353 (1678), *Works* 8:154. Cf. James 1:26f., and for 'a body of death' Romans 7:23.

6. A paper from 1654, in *Doctrinals, Works* 4:42. Cf. Jeremiah 14:14;

Ezekiel 13:6,7.

7. 'The vials of the wrath of God poured forth upon the Man of Sin' (1654), in *Doctrinals,Works* 4:30.

8. Epistle 392 (1684), *Works* 8:250. Cf. James 1:26f.

9. Epistle 357 (1679), *Works* 8:164.

10. From an account of his experience in 1647, in *Journal*, ed. John Nickalls, Cambridge University Press, 1952, p.13.

11. A paper of 1655, in *Journal*, ed. Ellwood, in *Works* 1:249. Cf. Joel 2:1,11; Amos 5:18.

12. 'The vials of the wrath of God poured forth upon the Man of Sin' (1654), in *Doctrinals,Works* 4:31. Cf. Luke 19:43f.

13. *Journal* (for 1647), ed. Ellwood, in *Works* 1:74. See Glossary on 'let' and 'experimental'.

14. *Journal* (for 1656), ed. Nickalls, p.277.

15. Quoted in Geoffrey Nuttall's Introduction, without date or reference, *Journal*, ed. Nickalls, p.xxvi. Cf. John 1:23.

16. 'A word from the Lord to all the world' (1654), in *Doctrinals, Works* 4:38.

17. Epistle 281 (1670), *Works* 8:31. Cf. Matthew 13:44-46.

18. Epistle 301 (1673), *Works* 8:52. Cf. 2 Corinthians 13:5.

19. A paper of 1657, in *Journal*, ed. Nickalls, p.310. Cf.1 Thessalonians 5:21.

20. *Journal* (for 1658), ed. Nickalls, p.345. 'These things' that occasioned bloodshed were the bread and wine of the eucharist, as is clear from the previous paragraph in the Journal.

21. Epistle 234 (1664), *Works* 7:256.

22. A paper to 'all professors' in 1654, in *Journal*, ed. Ellwood, in *Works* 1:215.

23. Epistle 19 (1652), *Works* 7:27.

24. Epistle 79 (1654), *Works* 7:89.

25. *Journal* (for 1647), ed. Ellwood, in *Works* 1:79.

26. *Journal* (for 1647), ed. Ellwood, in *Works* 1:77.

27. *Journal* (for 1648), ed. Ellwood, in *Works* 1:87.

28. Epistle 171 (1659), *Works* 7:159.

29. A paper of 1656, in *Journal*, ed. Ellwood, in *Works* 1:281. Cf. John 1:9; 1 John 2:26f. See Glossary on 'anointing'.

30. Epistle 222 (1662), *Works* 7:230.

31. Epistle 249 (1667), *Works* 7:291f. The story is from John 4:1-26.

32. Epistle 260 (1668), *Works* 7:316.

33. Epistle 249 (1667), *Works* 7:292.

34. Epistle 260 (1668), *Works* 7:317.

35. Epistle 65 (1654), *Works* 7:78.

36. Epistle 200 (1661), *Works* 7:193. On 'doing truth' cf. John 3:21; 1 John 1:6.

37. Epistle 289 (1671), *Works* 8:38.

38. Epistle 391 (1684), *Works* 8:248. Cf. Proverbs 23:23.

39. Epistle 220 (1662), *Works* 7:221.

40. Epistle 245 (1666), *Works* 7:275f. Cf. John 8:32.

41. Epistle 260 (1668), *Works* 7:311. Cf. John 8:32,36.

42. Epistle 178 (1659), *Works* 7:169.

43. A letter to Friends in 1671, in *Journal*, ed. Nickalls, pp.574f.

44. From the American diary, 1672, in *Journal*, ed. Nickalls, p.639.

45. *Journal* (for 1652), ed. Nickalls, p.135. Cf. Romans 1:26.

46. *Journal* (for 1663), ed. Nickalls, p.444.

47. *Journal* (for 1655), ed. Nickalls, p.212.

48. Epistle 172 (1659), *Works* 7:165. Cf. Genesis 3; John 8:44. See Glossary on 'original'.

49. Epistle 223 (1662), *Works* 7:238.

50. Epistle 355 (1679), *Works* 8:160.

51. *Journal* (for 1647), ed. Ellwood, in *Works* 1:77.

52. An epistle to Friends in the ministry, 1656, in *Journal*, ed. Ellwood, in *Works* 1:289.

53. Epistle 15 (1652), *Works* 7:23.

54. Epistle 16 (1652), *Works* 7:24f.

55. Epistle 35 (1653), *Works* 7:43.

56. Epistle 45 (1653), *Works* 7:56.

57. Epistle 234 (1664), *Works* 7:257.

58. Epistle 4 (1651), *Works* 7:18.

59. Epistle 56 (1653), *Works* 7:71f.

60. A paper of 1650, *Journal*, ed. Ellwood, in *Works* 1:108.

61. A letter to Lady Claypole, 1658, *Journal*, ed. Nickalls, pp.346f.

62. A letter to Oliver Cromwell, 1655, *Journal*, ed. Nickalls, p.194.

63. 'An epistle to all people on the earth' (1657), in *Doctrinals*, *Works* 4:132, checked by Hugh Ross against the copy of 1671 and with word order rearranged for clarity; see Hugh McGregor Ross, *George Fox speaks for himself*, Sessions, York, 1991, p.21.

64. Epistle 109 (1656), *Works* 7:116.

65. 'An epistle to all people on the earth' (1657), in *Doctrinals*, *Works* 4:125.

66. *Journal* (for 1653), ed. Nickalls, p.168. 'To sit under their vine' is a biblical image of peace (cf. Micah 4:3,4), but Fox may have had in mind (also) that Christ was called a vine (John 15:1,5).

67. Epistle 313 (1674), *Works* 8:72f.

68. Epistle 34 (1653), *Works* 7:42.

69. 'The voice of the Lord to the heathen', (1656), p.2; a tract not since published.

70. 'To the people of Uxbridge' (1659), *Doctrinals*, *Works* 4:207. Cf. Romans 1:19f.

71. From the American diary of 1672, in *Journal*, ed. Nickalls, p.642.

72. 'Truth's triumph in the eternal power over the dark inventions of fallen man' (1661), in *Doctrinals*, *Works* 4:284. Cf. John 16:7-13.

73. *The Great Mystery* (1659), in *Works* 3:518.

74. 'A word from the Lord to all the world' (1654?), in *Doctrinals*, *Works* 4:34.

75. *Journal* (for 1647), ed. Nickalls, p.14.

76. An epistle of 1652, in *Journal*, ed. Nickalls, p.144.

77. *Journal* (for 1648), ed. Nickalls, p.33. Cf. John 3:19; 12:36.

78. Journal (for 1652), ed. Nickalls, p.117.
79. Epistle 265 (1669), *Works* 8:7. The quotation is from Proverbs 4:18 (cf. 4:19). Cf. John 1:5.
80. Journal (for 1657), ed. Nickalls, p.303. Cf. John 1:1-3, 6-9.
81. Epistle 149 (1657), *Works* 7:142.
82. A paper of 1656, in Journal, ed. Ellwood, in *Works* 1:295.
83. A paper of 1654, in Doctrinals, *Works* 4:43.
84. Epistle 48 (1653), *Works* 7:61.
85. A paper of 1657, in Journal, ed. Ellwood, in *Works* 1:344.
86. Epistle 11 (1652), *Works* 7:21. See Glossary on 'naked'.
87. 'To the people of Uxbridge' (1659), in Doctrinals, *Works* 4:206.
88. Epistle 85 (1655), *Works* 7:96.
89. 'To all that would know the way to the kingdom' (1653), in Doctrinals, *Works* 4:17f. Cf. Joshua 1:7.
90. Epistle 10 (1652), *Works* 7:20. On 'the tempter' see Matthew 4:1-3 and Glossary on 'the devil'.
91. A letter to Lady Claypole, 1658, in Journal, ed. Nickalls, pp.347f.
92. 'A word from the Lord to all the world' (1654?), in Doctrinals, *Works* 4:38f. On 'the god of this world' see 2 Corinthians 4:4 and Glossary on 'the devil' and 'the world'.
93. Epistle 50 (1653), *Works* 7:66. Cf. Matthew 5:8.
94. Epistle 51 (1653), *Works* 7:67. Cf. Matthew 5:8.
95. Epistle 192 (1660), *Works* 7:183. The law in question is a moral law like the ten commandments. Cf. Galatians 3:19. On 'praise' see 1 Peter 2:13,14.
96. Epistle 184 (1659), *Works* 7:173.
97. Epistle 37 (1653), *Works* 7:45.
98. Epistle 259 (1668), *Works* 7:310. Cf. 1 John 1:7; 1 Timothy 6:16.
99. Epistle 249 (1667), *Works* 7:290f. Cf. Jeremiah 23:29: 'Is not my word like a fire? saith the Lord; and like a hammer that breaketh the rock in pieces?'; and Hebrews 4:12; 2 Corinthians 5:18f; 2 Peter 1:4; 1 Peter 1:24f (re. Isaiah 40:6). See Glossary

on 'the original'.

100. *Journal* (for 1655), ed. Nickalls, p.235. Cf. 1 Timothy 2:5.

101. Epistle 19 (1652), *Works* 7:27.

102. A letter to 'the Pope and all the Kings in Europe', 1655, in *Journal*, ed. Nickalls, p.205.

103. 'To the king of France' (1660), in *Doctrinals, Works* 4:237. Cf. 2 Corinthians 13:5.

104. Epistle 38 (1653), *Works* 7:47.

105. *Journal* (for 1648), ed. Ellwood, in *Works* 1:81.

106. 'A word from the Lord to all the world' (1654), in *Doctrinals, Works* 4:36f.

107. Epistle 189 (1659), *Works* 7:179. On 'the prince of life' see Acts 3:15.

108. Epistle 207 (1661), *Works* 7:207.

109. Epistle 230 (1663), *Works* 7:244.

110. Epistle 77 (1654), *Works* 7:87.

111. Epistle 209 (1661), *Works* 7:209.

112. Epistle 210 (1661), *Works* 7:210.

113. Epistle 89 (1655), *Works* 7:97.

114. Epistle 180 (1659), *Works* 7:170.

115. Epistle 181 (1659), *Works* 7:171.

116. Epistle 275 (1669), *Works* 8:19. The (rough) quotation is from Romans 10:10.

117. Epistle 206 (1661), *Works* 7:203.

118. Epistle 208 (1661), *Works* 7:208.

119. Epistle 216 (1662), *Works* 7:217.

120. Epistle 42 (1653), *Works* 7:51.

121. 'To the Turk' (1660), in *Doctrinals, Works* 4:219.

122. Epistle 55 (1653), *Works* 7:71.

123. An epistle to Friends, 1657, in *Journal*, ed. Ellwood, in *Works* 1:344.

124. Epistle 130 (1656), *Works* 7:123.

125. Epistle 155 (1657), *Works* 7:147.

126. Epistle 146 (1657), *Works* 7:138.

127. A letter to Lady Claypole, 1658, in *Journal*, ed. Nickalls, p.347. Cf. Job 13:4. On the 'glory of the first body' see 1 Corinthians 15: 38-40, 45, a reference to the creation of human beings (Genesis 2).

128. 'Christ is the Light of the World' (1654), an unpublished letter in the *Swarthmoor Manuscripts* of Fox's writings, vol. 17, no. 136, Friends House Library, London; printed as a single page leaflet by the Wider Quaker Fellowship of Philadelphia in 1987, and partly reprinted in T Canby Jones, ed., *The power of the Lord is over all: the pastoral letters of George Fox*, Friends United Press, Richmond, Indiana, 1989, p.477.

129. Epistle 31 (1653), *Works* 7:37f.

130. Epistle 264 (1669), *Works* 7:348.

131. Epistle 196 (1660), *Works* 7:187.

ANTHOLOGY
part 2: *the group*

SEEING OTHERS

1 Abiding inwardly in the light, it will let you see one another and the unity with one another.

2 Ye that are turned to the light, and gathered into it, meet together, and keep your meetings, that ye may feel and see the life of God among you, and know that in one another.

3 Mind the light, that all may be refreshed one in another, and all in one. And the God of power and love keep all Friends in power, in love, that there be no surmisings, but pure refreshings in the unlimited love of God, which makes one another known in the conscience, to read one another's hearts: being comprehended into this love, it is inseparable, and all are here one.

4 And take heed of presumption, lest ye go from the living God; but in the spirit dwell... And this brings you to see and read one another, as epistles written in one another's hearts, where in unity, love, and peace ye will come to dwell.

5 Mind that which is eternal, which gathers your hearts together up to the Lord, and lets you see that ye are written in one another's hearts; meet together everywhere.

6 And know the life of God in one another, and the power of God in one another; but that knowledge in the form without the life we deny, though it be never so finely painted, and the harlot be never so beautiful.

MEETING

7 When that ye are met together in the light, hearken to it, that ye may feel the power of God in every one of you. So here comes your ear to be opened to hear the

SEEING OTHERS

1 As you live with the light in yourselves it will enable you to see one another, and the unity between you.

2 You who are now facing the light and gathered together in it, be sure you meet together and keep on meeting so that you experience the life of God among you and recognise it in one another.

3 Keeping your mind on the light you will all be a source of refreshment to one another, both individually and together. So may the God of power and love maintain you all in power and love so that, instead of finding fault with one another, you will refresh one another in the unlimited love of God. For it is this love that enables you to be truly aware of one another, to read one another's hearts. So being held together in this love you cannot be separated from it, or divided among yourselves.

4 And beware of arrogance, in case it leads you away from the living God. Rather, live with the spirit... and this will enable you to be aware of one another, and to read one another as if you were letters written on one another's hearts. And in that awareness you will come to live in unity, love and peace.

5 Give attention to what is eternal, because that gathers your hearts together, brings them closer to the Lord and lets you see that you are written on one another's hearts. Meet together wherever you are.

6 And get to know the life of God in one another, and the power of God in one another. But that formal kind of knowledge which lacks the [inner] life we repudiate, however finely it is painted, however beautiful the prostitute may be!

MEETING

7 When you are met together in the light, listen to it so that you may counsel of the Lord God; and here the eye comes to be opened to see the Lord Jesus Christ in the midst of you.

8 Christ Jesus... you may see the beginning of his setting up his meetings, when he saith, 'Where two or three are gathered together in my name, I am in the midst of them.'

9 Since the days of the apostles, the true church hath been in the wilderness, and the beast, false prophet, antichrist, and false church have ruled and reigned.

10 The steeple-houses and pulpits were offensive to my mind, because both priest and people called them the house of God, and idolized them; reckoning that God dwelt in the outward house. Whereas they should have looked for God and Christ to dwell in their hearts, and their bodies to be made the temples of God.

11 Few at the first took care for the establishing men and women's meetings, though they were generally owned when they understood them: but the everlasting God, that sent me forth by his everlasting power, first to declare his everlasting gospel; and then after people had received the gospel, I was moved to go through the nation, to advise them to set up the men's meetings, and the women's, many of which were set up.

12 The thing is this: that if you had (once in a year) a Yearly Meeting... for Friends to see one another, and know how the affairs of truth prosper, and how Friends do grow in the truth of God, to the comfort and joy of one another in it... all things (by the truth and power of God) may be kept in peace and love, all dwelling in the wisdom of God.

WORSHIP

13 You may petition the emperor or king, and your patrons, whose captives you are, that you may have

sense the power of God in every one of you. In doing this you will find your ear being tuned to hear the counsel of the Lord God, and your eye being opened to see the Lord Jesus Christ among you.

8 Christ Jesus… you can see when he first set up his meetings, when he said 'where two or three are gathered together in my name I am among them'.

9 Ever since the days of the apostles the true church has been in the wilderness, whilst 'the beast', the false prophet, the opponent of Christ and the false church have all held sway.

10 The steeple houses and pulpits were offensive to my mind because the priest and people both called them 'the house of God' and idolised them, reckoning that God lived in a literal house, whereas what they should have done is to look to have God and Christ living in their hearts, and to have their own bodies made the temples of God.

11 Few at first showed interest in establishing men's and women's meetings, though they were generally owned when they were understood. But the everlasting God, who sent me out by his everlasting power first to declare his everlasting gospel, then, after people had received the gospel, moved me to go through the nation to advise them to set up the men's meetings and the women's, many of which were set up.

12 The thing is this: if you had a yearly meeting, just once a year… for Friends to see one another and learn how the affairs of truth are prospering and how Friends are growing in the truth of God, so that you might be comforted and heartened by one another in this… then everything – by the truth and power of God – would be kept in peace and love, since you would all be living according to God's wisdom.

WORSHIP

13 You may petition the emperor or king, and your patrons who hold you captive, that you may have one day in the week to meet together

one day in the week to meet together to worship and serve the great God (that made you) in spirit and truth. For you worship no representation, image or likeness, neither in heaven nor in the earth, but the great God who is Lord over all, both in heaven and earth, and is manifest by his spirit in his people.

14 This worship in the spirit and in the truth hits all men and women; they must come to the spirit in themselves, and the truth in the inward parts; this is public, this is not a private worship... in which spirit and truth they must bow down, and come into it, if they be worshippers of God in the truth and in the spirit.... They must come to the truth in the heart, to the hidden man in the heart, to a meek and quiet spirit.

15 Friends, be watchful and careful in all meetings ye come into. When a man is come newly out of the world he cometh out of the dirt. Then he must not be rash. For now when he cometh into a silent meeting, that is another state. Then he must come and feel his own spirit how it is, when he cometh to those that sit silent; for he may come in the heat of his spirit out of the world.... Friends, come into that which is over all the spirits of the world, with that ye may see where others stand, and reach that which is of God in everyone.

16 Wait to know the time of silence.

17 Your growth in the seed is in the silence.

UNITY

18 All they that are in the light are in unity; for the light is but one....

   All who know the word, which is a mystery, are come to the beginning, are sanctified by the word, and clean through the word;... and this is a word of reconciliation, that reconcileth together to God, and gathers the hearts of

to worship and wait in spirit and truth on the great God who made you. For you don't worship a representation, image or likeness, either in heaven or on earth; you worship the great God who is lord over all, both in heaven and on earth, and who is manifest by his spirit in his people.

14 This 'worship in the spirit and in the truth' (John 4:23,24) touches every man and woman: they each have to come to the spirit in themselves, and come to the truth in their own inner being. And this is public worship we're speaking about, not private. If they are really to 'worship God in the truth and in the spirit', they have to surrender in spirit and truth and enter into them [personally]....They have to come to the truth in the heart, to the hidden self in the heart, and to a humble and quiet spirit.

15 Friends, be alert and careful in every meeting you attend. When a man has only recently left the ways of the world, for example, he still carries the dirt of the world with him. So he must not act rashly. For when he now comes into a silent meeting, he is entering a different state [of being]. So when he joins the others sitting in silence he should become aware of how he is in himself, in his spirit, because he may well have an over-heated state of mind from his experience of the world.... Friends, enter that state of mind which transcends all worldly concerns, and in that state you will be able to see where other people are and be able to reach that part in everyone that is part of God.

16 Wait till you experience the time of silence.

17 Your growth from the seed takes place in the silence.

UNITY

18 All those who live in the light are one, because the light itself is one.... All those who know the word, though it is a mystery, have experienced the origin [of everything]. They are purified by the word and made clean.... And this is a word of reconciliation, because it reconciles [people] to God and gathers the hearts of his people together to live in love and unity with one another. And it lets them see how

his together, to live in love and unity one with another, and lets them see how they have been strangers and aliens from the life of God.... Abiding inwardly in the light, it will let you see one another and the unity one with another.

19 All ye that are turned unto this living way by the power of the mighty God of heaven and earth, live in peace one with another, and unity; and do not judge one another, for that eats and wears out the good, and begets the enmity; and hinders growth in truth.... And so it will be your life to do good, and to beget into life, up to God; and in that power, that doth so, ye will not labour in vain. But above all things take heed of judging one another, for in that ye may destroy one another, and leave one another behind, and drive one another back into the world, and eat out the good of one another; and so hinder unity, hinder growth in the life and the power of God, in which ye should have peace and joy in one another, and love, which edifies and overcomes and gets the victory.

20 Let the weight and preciousness of truth be in your eye, and esteemed above all things by you. For here is my grief, when I hear any thing amongst Friends that hinders their unity, and makes a breach.

21 As people come into subjection to the spirit of God, and grow up in the image and power of the Almighty, they may receive the word of wisdom that opens all things, and come to know the hidden unity in the eternal being.

22 So Friends are not to meet like a company of people about town or parish business, neither in their men's nor women's meetings, but to wait upon the Lord, and feeling his power and spirit to lead them, and order them to his glory, that so whatsoever they may do, they may do it to the praise and glory of God, and in unity in the faith and in the spirit and in fellowship in the order of the gospel.

they have been estranged and alienated from the life of God.... As you live with the light in yourselves it will enable you to see one another, and the unity between you.

19 All you who have been led into this living way by the power of the mighty God of heaven and earth, see to it that you live in peace with one another and in unity. Don't criticise one another, for that only eats up the good and wears it out, generating hostility and hindering growth in the truth.... So your life will be about doing good, generating life [in others] and bringing them close to God. And the power that enables you to live like this will ensure that you do not labour in vain. But above everything else take care not to criticise one another, for that way you can destroy one another, or abandon one another, or drive one another back into the ways of the world. And you will eat up the good in one another and so hinder unity, hinder growth in the life and the power of God. And it's that life and power that would give you peace and joy in one another, and love, and would strengthen you and enable you to overcome and gain the victory.

20 Keep in mind how weighty and precious the truth is. Value it above everything else. For this is what gives me grief, when I hear that something among Friends is hindering their unity and causing a breach.

21 As people surrender to the spirit of God and with his help grow into the image of the Almighty they can receive the word of wisdom that opens up everything and discover the hidden unity in the eternal Being.

22 So, Friends are not to meet like a group of people about town or parish business, either in their men's or women's meetings. They are to wait on the Lord, sensing his power and spirit to lead them and to establish an order among them that will bring credit to him. Then, whatever they do, they will be able to do it to bring praise and credit to God, and they will do it together, united in faith and in the spirit, and in the fellowship made possible by the order of the gospel.

GOSPEL ORDER

23 The apostle said to the church, 'Let all things be done decently and in order'.... So this was the spiritual order of the gospel.

24 For what order can there be in the world's god, and amongst his subjects, in whom there is no truth? For in whom there is no truth, there is no true order; and they that abide not in the truth, grace, light, spirit, gospel faith and word of life, they abide not in the order of God and Christ.

25 For all our men's and women's meetings, which are set up by the power and spirit of God, these meetings are for the practice of religion, and to see that all that do profess truth, do practise it and walk in it.

26 You who have received Christ, have received power to become the sons of God, and to believe in the light... therefore I say unto you, let no man abuse this power, that is everlasting; and keep the gospel order... so that in all your men's and women's meetings, see that virtue flow, and see that all your words be gracious, and see that love flows, which bears all things, that kindness, tenderness, and gentleness may be among you, and that the fruits of the good spirit may abound.... For you have the light to see all evil, and the power to withstand it, and to see that nothing be lacking.

27 The authority of our meetings is the power of God, the gospel which brings life and immortality to light, that they may see over the devil that has darkened them, and that all the heirs of the gospel might walk according to the gospel, and glorify God with their bodies, souls and spirits, which are the Lord's. And so the order of the glorious gospel is not of man nor by man.

28 And women are to keep the comely order of the gospel, as well as men.

GOSPEL ORDER

23 The apostle said to the church, 'Let everything be done decently and in order'.… So this was the spiritual order of the gospel.

24 For what order can there be under the rule of this world's god, or among his subjects, when there is no truth in them? For where there is no truth, there is no true order either. And those who don't live by the truth, grace, light, spirit, gospel faith and word of life, they don't live by the order of God and Christ.

25 For all our men's and women's meetings that have been set up by the power and spirit of God, these are meetings for the practice of religion, to see that everyone who professes truth puts it into practice and lives by it.

26 You who have received Christ have received power to become the sons of God and to believe in the light.… Therefore I say to you, let no one abuse this power that lasts forever. And maintain the gospel order… so that in all your men's and women's meetings virtue may flow, your words may all be gracious, and love may flow – love that bears with everything. Then kindness, tenderness and gentleness will be among you and the fruits of the good spirit will abound… For you have the light to see all that's wrong, and the power to resist it and to see that nothing is lacking.

27 The authority of our meetings is the power of God. And that power lies in 'the gospel… which brings life and immortality to light' (2 Timothy 1:10) so that people may be able to see through the darkness that the devil has brought on them and that, having accepted the promise of the gospel, they will be able to live their lives in accordance with it, bringing credit to God in all that they are, body, soul and spirit, since all that they are belongs to him. So the order of the glorious gospel is not designed or constructed by human beings.

28 And women are to maintain this wonderful order of the gospel, just as the men are.

29 From thence we passed... into the South Hams... where we had some of all the men Friends together, and there settled the Men's Monthly Meetings in the heavenly order of the gospel, the power of God, which answered the power of God in all.

WOMEN AND MEN

30 Now when the women are met together in the light and in the gospel, the power of God, some are of a more large capacity and understanding than other women, and are able to inform and instruct and stir up others into diligence, virtue and righteousness... and to help them that be of weaker capacities and understandings in the wisdom of God, that they may be fruitful in every good work and word.

31 Hath not every one their service that are enlightened?

32 But what spirit is this, that would exercise lordship over the faith of any? And what a spirit is this, that will neither suffer the women to speak amongst the men, nor to meet amongst themselves to speak? But all this is for judgment, with that spirit that gives liberty unto all that labour in the gospel, in the light and in the grace.... For the power and spirit of God gives liberty to all, for women are heirs of life as well as the men, and heirs of grace and of the light of Christ Jesus as well as the men, and so stewards of the manifold grace of God.

33 Some men may say, man must have the power and superiority over the woman, because God says, 'The man must rule over his wife, and that man is not of the woman, but the woman is of the man'. Indeed, after man fell that command was, but before man fell there was no such command, for they were both meet-helps and they were both to have dominion over all that God made. And as the

29 From there we passed… into South Hams… where we met together with some of the men Friends, and there we set up the Men's Monthly Meetings according to the divine order of the gospel. And since the gospel is God's own power the Meetings responded to the experience of God's power in everyone.

WOMEN AND MEN

30 Now when the women are met together in the light and in the gospel, which is God's power, [it is evident that] some have a greater capacity and understanding than other women, and that they are able to inform and instruct and inspire others to apply themselves and to do what is right and virtuous… and to help those with less capacity and understanding to grasp the wisdom of God, so that they may become fruitful in every good thing that they say and do.

31 Doesn't everyone who is enlightened have something to offer?

32 But what spirit is this that wants to exercise authority over the faith of someone else? And what spirit is this that won't allow the women to speak among the men, or even to speak among themselves? All this has to be exposed by that very different spirit that gives liberty to everyone who works in the gospel, and in the light, and in the grace.… For the power and spirit of God give liberty to everyone, for women have received God's gift of life as well as men, and they have received grace and the light of Christ Jesus as well as the men. So they too are stewards of the varied gifts given them by God.

33 Some men may say that a man must have the power and superiority over the woman, because God says, 'the man must rule over his wife' (Genesis 3:16), and 'the man is not derived from the woman, but the woman from the man' (1 Corinthians 11:8). Indeed there was such a command after the humans fell, but before they fell there was no such command, because they were companions to each other and they were both to have dominion over all that God had made. And as the apostle says, 'if woman was made from man' – his next words are – 'so man

apostle saith, 'for as the woman is of the man', his next words are, 'so is the man also by the woman; but all things are of God'. And so the apostle clears his own words; and so as man and woman are restored again by Christ up into the image of God, they both have dominion again in right-eousness and holiness and are helps-meet, as before they fell.

34 And may not the spirit of Christ speak in the female as well as in the male? Is he there to be limited? Who is it that dare limit the holy one of Israel? For the light is the same in the male and in the female, which cometh from Christ, he by whom the world was made, and so Christ is one in all and not divided; and who is it that dare stop Christ's mouth?

MINISTRY

35 Let not the sons and daughters, nor the handmaids, be stopped in their prophesyings, nor the young men in their visions, nor the old men in their dreams.... So every one may improve their talents, every one exercise their gifts, and every one speak as the spirit gives them utterance. Thus every one may minister, as he hath received the grace, as a good steward to him that hath given it him; so that all plants may bud, and 'bring forth fruit' to the glory of God.

36 Take heed of many words; what reacheth to the life settles in the life. That which cometh from the life, and is received from God, reacheth to the life, and settles others in the life: the work is not now as it was at first; the work now is to settle and stay in the life.... For if Friends do not live in the pure life which they speak of, to answer the life in those they speak to, the other part steps in; and so there comes up an outward acquaintance, and he lets that come over him.... When all are settled in the life they are in that which remains for ever; and what is received there, is received from the Lord; and what one receiveth from the Lord, he

is also made from woman, but God is the source of all' (1 Corinthians
11:12). So the apostle clarifies what he said [in v.8]. And so, as man
and woman are restored by Christ to 'the image of God' [they were
made to be, Genesis 1:27], they both have dominion again as companions together, as they had before they fell, exercising power
according to what is right and holy.

34 Can't the spirit of Christ speak in the female as well as in the male?
Or is he to be limited in that respect? And who would take it on
himself to 'set the limit for the holy one of Israel' (Psalm 78:41)? For
the light is the same in the male and in the female. And it comes from
Christ, the one through whom the world itself was made. So Christ is
one in all and not split up. And who dares tell Christ to stop talking?

MINISTRY

35 Don't let your sons and daughters, or your servant-girls, be hindered
in their prophesying, or the young men in their visions, or the old
men in their dreams.... In this way everyone may improve their
talents, exercise their gifts and speak as the spirit gives them power to
do so. So everyone can minister as they are given grace, as good stewards of the one who gives them grace, so that all the plants may bud
and yield fruit to the glory of God.

36 Beware of too much talk: whatever touches the life [within them]
will establish them in that life. What initially comes from the life
[within you] and is received from God, that will touch the life in
others and establish them in the life. The work we have to do now is
not quite what it was at first – the work now is to establish [Friends]
in the life and to remain in it.... For if Friends don't live in the pure
life they talk about, to resonate with the life in those they are talking
to, then something else in them takes over – their understanding
becomes superficial.... When everyone is established in the life they
have something that lasts forever. And whatever anyone receives in
that place they receive from the Lord, and what anyone receives from
the Lord is theirs to keep. So they sit still, cool and quiet in their own

keepeth; so he sitteth still, cool and quiet in his own spirit, and gives it forth as he is moved.

37 It is a weighty thing to be in the work of the ministry of the Lord God, and to go forth in that. It is not as a customary preaching; it is to bring people to the end of all outward preaching.

FORMS

38 Awake, awake all people everywhere who live in forms, see what ye possess, not having that eternal spirit that gave forth the scriptures; all your formal prayers, formal preaching, formal singing, will be found as the chaff, which is for the unquenchable fire.

39 The conscience being seared, there is a returning to teachers without. For the carnal will have its vain invented form; but the spirit's form stands in the power. Prove yourselves where ye are.

40 Christendom have more minded the hireling's voice, than Christ the light's voice, the truth's voice, the voice of the life and power of God in themselves.

41 To all you that are unlearned outwardly, of the letter, that cannot read the scripture outwardly, to you I have a word from the Lord to speak; which is, Christ saith, I have given to every one a measure, according to their ability; this is the measure, the light which is pure, which doth convince thee, and if thou dost take heed to this light, that is scripture within thee.

42 Old Adam's sons and daughters may get the words of Christ, and of the prophets and apostles, but are out of their life, as their practice speaks. And therefore it is the life that differs, and the new way differs from the old, and the religion that is above from that which is below; and the

spirit, and they give it out to others only as they are moved to do so.

37 It's a serious matter to be involved in the ministry of the Lord God, and to go travelling in it. It's not the usual kind of preaching. In fact it is intended to bring an end to all preaching that depends on a formal structure.

FORMS

38 Wake up, wake up all of you anywhere who live in [a dreamworld of] forms. Look what you've got when you don't have the eternal spirit that gave you the scriptures. All your formal prayers, formal preaching, formal singing will be found to be nothing but chaff, fit only for the unquenchable fire.

39 Their conscience having been scorched, they turn back to teachers outside them. For the sensual part of us wants a humanly devised form of its own, empty though it is. But the form created by the spirit rests on something else, on 'the power' (2 Timothy 3:5). Test yourselves as to where you are.

40 Christian society has paid more attention to the voice of the hired man than to the voice of Christ the light, the voice of truth, the voice of the life and power of God in themselves.

41 To all of you who lack an education, formally speaking, who can't read the scriptures as a book, I have something to say to you, a word from the Lord: Christ says, 'I have given to everyone a portion of the light which is pure, according to their ability'. This is what convinces you [of the truth], and if you pay attention to it, the light, then that is scripture in you.

42 Men and women in a fallen condition, like old Adam, may well know the words of Christ, and the words of the prophets and apostles, but they know nothing of the life from which the words come, as we can see from the way they live. So it's the life that makes the difference, and that is how the new way differs from the old, the religion above from

worship Christ set up above sixteen hundred years ago, from all them that are made since amongst the nominal christians.

43 Heed not words without life.

SCRIPTURE

44 At one time there came three nonconformist priests and two lawyers to discourse with me; and one of the priests undertook to prove that the scriptures are the only rule of life. Whereupon, after I had plunged him about his proof, I had a fit opportunity to open unto them the right and proper use, service and excellency of the scriptures; and also to show that the spirit of God… is the most fit, proper and universal rule, which God hath given to all mankind to rule, direct, govern and order their lives by.

45 This I was moved to declare, that the scriptures were given forth by the spirit of God and all people must first come to the spirit of God in themselves by which they might know God and Christ, of whom the prophets and the apostles learnt; and by the same spirit they might know the holy scriptures and the spirit which was in them that gave them forth; so that spirit of God must be in them that come to know them again.

46 The people had the scriptures but they were not turned to the spirit which should let them see that which gave them forth, which is the key to open them, the spirit of God.

47 They could not know the spiritual meaning of Moses, the prophets and John's words, nor see their path and travels, much less to see through them and to the end of them into the kingdom, unless they had the spirit and light of Jesus; nor could they know the words of Christ and of his apostles without his spirit. But as man comes through by the

the religion below, and the religion that Christ established over sixteen hundred years ago from all those that have been made since among the nominal Christians.

43 Don't listen to words that have no life in them.

SCRIPTURE

44 Once I had a visit from three nonconformist ministers and two lawyers who wanted to talk with me. One of the ministers took it on himself to prove that the scriptures were the only guide to life, which gave me the opportunity, once I had demolished his proof, to explain to them the right and proper use of the scriptures and how they were to be valued and brought to bear on life. And also to show that the most appropriate and universal guide was the spirit of God, which God had given to all human beings to guide, direct, order and run their lives by.

45 I was moved to say this, that the scriptures emanated from the spirit of God and that people must first come to the spirit of God in themselves so that they can get to know God and Christ, which is essentially what the prophets and apostles [who wrote the scriptures] had themselves come to know. Then, with the help of the spirit which gives them this knowledge, they will get to know the holy scriptures and the spirit in those people who wrote them. So, people now who want to know for themselves what they knew then must have that spirit of God within them.

46 The people had the scriptures in their possession but they had not turned to the spirit which would have let them see where they came from, the spirit of God itself, which is the key to open them.

47 They could not know the spiritual meaning of Moses' words, or of the prophets' and John's words, nor see the path and the journey they had travelled, much less see the end of that path in the kingdom, unless they had the spirit and light of Jesus. Nor could they understand the words of Christ and of his apostles without the help of his spirit. But as people come through to Christ by the spirit and power of God...

spirit and power of God to Christ... and is led by the holy
ghost into the truth and substance of the scriptures, sitting
down in him who is the author and end of them, then are
they read and understood with profit and great delight.

48 These things I did not see by the help of man, nor by the
letter, though they are written in the letter; but I saw them in
the light of the Lord Jesus Christ, and by his immediate spirit
and power, as did the holy men of God by whom the holy
scriptures were written. Yet I had no slight esteem of the holy
scriptures, they were very precious to me. For I was in that
spirit by which they were given forth; and what the Lord
opened in me, I afterwards found was agreeable to them.

49 The Lord had said to me, 'If but one man or woman were
raised by his power, to stand and live in the same spirit that
the prophets and apostles were in who gave forth the scriptures, that man or woman should shake all the country in
their profession for ten miles round'.

AUTHORITY

50 They came to see and feel that the power of God was the
authority of their meetings.

51 Keep your habitations and your first love, and do not go
forth from your rule of faith and life within; in which you
all have unity and fellowship.... And if you do not go forth
from the light, spirit and truth within, the light you will feel
to guide and lead you, and instruct you.

DISCERNMENT

52 Watch over one another that with that which is pure ye
may discern and have unity with that which is pure.

53 Keep... in your habitations of the light, life and power of

and are led by the holy spirit into the truth and reality of the scriptures, sitting at the feet of the one by whom and for whom they were written, the scriptures can be read and understood with profit and great delight.

48 I did not understand these things with human resources, or with the help of books, though they are written down in a book, but I understood them in the light of the Lord Jesus Christ and by his immediate spirit and power, as had those holy people of God by whom the holy scriptures had been written. Yet I had no little esteem for the holy scriptures; they were very precious to me. For I was living in that spirit which led them to be written in the first place. And what the Lord opened up to me I found later to be consistent with them.

49 The Lord had said to me that if just one man or woman were to be raised up by his power to stand and live in the same spirit that the prophets and apostles had lived in when they wrote the scriptures, that man or woman would shake everyone in their belief for ten miles around.

AUTHORITY

50 They came to see and feel that it was that power of God that was the authority in their meetings.

51 Stay at home, stay with your first love, and do not leave your guide to faith and life within you. This is where you find unity and fellowship.... And if you do not leave the light, spirit and truth within, you will feel the light guide you and lead you, and instruct you.

DISCERNMENT

52 Watch over one another so that you may come to discern with the help of that part of you which is pure and to live in harmony with it.

53 Stay... in your home of the light, life and power of God – this is what

God (the gospel), by which you all see and discern your own conditions with the spirit of discerning, laying hand on no man suddenly, but proving and trying all things, seeing your own conditions by the power of the Lord and his light, by which ye may have the spirit of discerning, waiting and walking in the truth.

54 Dear father and mother in the flesh... to that of God in you both I speak, and do beseech you both for the Lord's sake to return within, and wait to hear the voice of the Lord there; and waiting there and keeping close to the Lord, a discerning will grow, that ye may distinguish the voice of the stranger, when ye hear it.

55 My desire is that you all may be kept in the power and spirit of God and Christ in humility, and in that you will have a sense of all things, that whatever you act it may be done in the spirit and power of Jesus Christ to the praise of God the Father, who is over all, from everlasting to everlasting, who beholds and sees all your words and actions, that you may behold and see with his spirit.

PRACTICE

56 My desire is that all may be kept in his power and spirit faithful to God and man, first to God in obeying him in all things and secondly in doing unto all men that which is just and righteous, true and holy and honest, to all men and women in all things that they have to do with or deal withal with them, that the Lord God may be glorified in the practising truth, holiness, godliness and righteousness amongst them, in all their lives and conversations.

57 This is the word of the Lord God to you all, keep down, keep low, that nothing may rule nor reign in you but life itself.

58 If you want wisdom, keep in the truth.

is meant by the gospel (Romans 1:16) – which enable you to see and discern your own condition with the spirit of discernment. Don't be hasty in 'laying hands on anyone' (1 Timothy 5:22), but try things out and put them to the test, looking to your own condition with the help of the Lord's power and light, which will give you the spirit of discernment, and waiting in and acting on the truth.

54 Dear father and mother [naturally speaking],... I want to speak to that part of you both which comes from God: please, both of you, for the Lord's sake, go back inside and wait there to hear the voice of the Lord. And as you wait there and keep close to the Lord your discernment will grow. You will then be able to distinguish 'the voice of the stranger' (John 10:5), should you also hear that.

55 My desire is that you may all be kept in humble dependence on the power and spirit of God and Christ, and that through that you will gain such a sense of things that whatever you do it will be done in the spirit and power of Jesus Christ to the praise of God the Father, who transcends everything and always has and always will, who looks and sees everything you say and do, so that you in turn may look and see with the help of his spirit.

PRACTICE

56 My desire is that, with the help of his power and spirit, everyone will remain faithful to God and humans: to God first of all, by obeying him in everything, and then secondly, to human beings, doing to all men and women that they have anything to do with or have any dealings with, only what is just and right, true and holy and honest, so that glory may go to God in the way they live their lives, in the way they put truth into practice and pursue what is holy and sacred and right.

57 This is what the Lord God has to say to you all: be humble, be accepting, so that nothing may rule your lives but life itself.

58 If you lack wisdom stay with the truth.

59 Dwell in the truth.

60 Though you may be convinced of the truth... they are happy that do obey the truth of what they are convinced; and if they do not, they will lose the days of their innocency and simplicity.

61 And therefore in the truth live... and that truth makes you free. In which truth and spirit is God worshipped.

62 So in all husbandry speak truth, act truth, doing justly and uprightly in all your actions, in all your practices, in all your words, in all your dealings, buyings, sellings, changings and commerce with people, let truth be the head and practise it.

63 The sun shines and the light is clear, and not dim, that you may see your way, and life, though there is a storm and tempest in the sea.

64 Now in this holy seed is the treasure of wisdom and knowledge, and as you all live and walk in this seed, you will have wisdom and knowledge that is heavenly from this treasure; with which wisdom and knowledge you will have understanding, that all your conversations may be ordered by it aright... and all your words may be gracious, and seasoned with grace; and whatever promises you may make to any man, you may consider before, that you may perform them... that so you may be lights of the world, and the salt of the earth, that... you may be instrumental to open the eyes of others.

65 In the meantime, while ye are... taking notice of others' cruelty, tyranny and persecution, turn your eye upon yourselves, and see what ye are doing at home. To the light of Christ Jesus in all your consciences I speak, which cannot lie, nor err, nor bear false witness; but doth bear witness for

59 Make your home in the truth.

60 Even though you are convinced of the truth… you will be happy only when you obey the truth you are convinced of. And if you don't, you will surely lose your chance of innocence and simplicity.

61 And therefore live with the truth… and that truth will then set you free. And with that truth and spirit you will be able to worship God.

62 In whatever work you do to make a living speak the truth, act on the truth, do what is just and right in all your actions, in all your practices, in all your words, in all your buying, selling, exchanging and commercial dealings with people. Let truth be your first concern and put it into practice.

63 The sun is shining and the light is bright enough for you to see your way, to see your life, even though there is a violent storm at sea.

64 Now in this holy seed is to be found the treasure of wisdom and knowledge, and as you draw your life from this seed you will gain spiritual wisdom and knowledge from this treasure. And from that in turn you will gain an understanding that enables you to conduct your lives rightly… and to speak always graciously, that your words may be 'seasoned with grace' (Colossians 4:6). It will ensure too that whatever promises you make to anyone you will be able to consider beforehand how they can be carried out…. In this way you will become lights for the world, salt for the earth (Matthew 5:13-16), and thus… instrumental in opening the eyes of others.

65 In the meantime, while you are… taking note of other people's cruelty, tyranny and persecution you might turn your eye on yourselves and see what you are doing at home. Let me speak to the light of Christ Jesus which exists in the conscience of every one of you, and which is incapable of telling lies, making mistakes or bearing false witness: it bears witness for God and appeals to you to act fairly, justly and rightly.

God, and cries for equity, justice and righteousness to be executed.

66 In the light walk, and ye will shine.

WORDS

67 In the power ye will all come to feel the end of words, the life, from which all words of truth were given forth.

68 And take heed of words without life, for they tend to draw you out of the power to live above the truth, and out of your conditions; which nature will not have peace, except it have words.

69 Mind not words without the power, nor the pleasing of the reason and carnal knowledge, wisdom and understanding, of fancies and thoughts of men.

70 People must not be always talking and hearing, but they must come into obedience.

71 There are too many talkers, and few walkers in Christ.

INTEGRITY

72 I do charge you all in the presence of the living God to dwell in what ye speak and profess; and none to profess what he doth not dwell in; and none to profess what he is not.

73 Take heed of knowledge, for it puffeth up, but dwell in the truth, and be what ye speak.

74 Mind that which first convinced you, that power of God which first awakened you, and arise and live in it, that all your eyes, minds and hearts may be kept single and naked

66 Walk in the light and you will shine.

WORDS

67 In the experience of the power you will all come to realise what words are for, namely the life from which all words of truth [ultimately] come.

68 And beware of words that have no life in them, for they tend to draw you away from the experience of the power and into a life cut off from truth, cut off from the reality of your own experience. In that condition you can never be satisfied unless you have words.

69 Pay no attention to words that have no power in them, or to words meant to please the reason and the merely human kind of knowledge, wisdom and understanding, or to words that appeal to human fancies and thoughts.

70 People should not always be talking and hearing – they should learn to obey.

71 Too many people can talk about Christ, while few walk the way of Christ.

INTEGRITY

72 In the presence of the living God let me tell you all what your responsibility is: it is to live your daily life in the reality you speak about and profess to believe in, and not to profess to believe in what you don't live out in practice, and not to profess to be what you are not.

73 Beware of knowledge, it can make you conceited, but live with the truth and be what you say you are.

74 Keep your mind on what first convinced you, that power of God which first awakened you, and get up and live in it! You will then be kept honest and sincere in your minds, and your hearts will be open, to God, and to one another, and unclothed of all that is contrary.

75 We have not, as some others, gone about cunningly with devised fables, nor have we ever denied in practice what we have professed in principle; but in sincerity and truth and by the word of God have we laboured to be made manifest unto all men, that both we and our ways might be witnessed in the hearts of all. And whereas all manner of evil hath been falsely spoken of us, we hereby speak the plain truth of our hearts, to take away the occasion of that offence, that so we being innocent may not suffer for other men's offences, nor be made a prey upon by the wills of men for that of which we were never guilty; but in the uprightness of our hearts we may, under the power ordained of God for the punishment of evil-doers, and for the praise of them that do well, live a peaceable life in all godliness and honesty.

VIRTUE

76 Be kind and courteous one towards another, all studying to be quiet, and to excel one another in virtue and purity and holiness and righteousness and godliness, in all your words and lives and conversations; so that you may all walk as become saints and christians, every one esteeming and preferring one another above yourselves in the truth, in meekness and lowliness of mind and humility; for he that inhabits eternity dwells with an humble heart. And therefore, do not quench the least motion of God's good spirit in yourselves, nor in any other; but let truth and goodness be cherished in all; and let all harshness and bitterness and revilings be kept down by the truth, that it may have its passage through you all, and in it you may bear one another's weakness and infirmities.... Therefore be careful, fervent, circumspect and faithful in the truth, and let your moderation, temperance and sobriety appear to all men,

naked before God and before one another, stripped of everything that is contrary to them.

75 We have not, like some, gone about telling cleverly concocted tales, nor have we ever denied in practice what we professed in principle, but in all sincerity and honesty and by God speaking [in us] we have worked hard to be clearly visible to everyone, so that everyone in their hearts might witness what we are and how we live. And because many bad things have been said about us, falsely, we want to state here the plain truth of our hearts so that it may be seen that those criticisms have no basis in fact, and that, since we ourselves are innocent, we should not have to suffer for the wrongs of others or be preyed upon for something of which we were never guilty. Then perhaps, given the integrity of our hearts and a government ordered by God 'for the punishment of those who do wrong and the commendation of those who do right' (1 Peter 2:14), we may be able to live a peaceable life devoted to God and truth.

VIRTUE

76 Be kind and courteous towards one another, learning how to be quiet, how to excel in virtue and purity in everything you say and do so that your whole lives may be devoted to what is sacred and right, in a way fitting for saints and Christians. Let everyone, in humility, reckon others more advanced in the truth than they are, for 'the one who inhabits eternity... lives with a humble heart' (Isaiah 57:15). And therefore, do not stifle the least prompting of God's good spirit in yourselves, or in others, but value truth and goodness, and let truth itself subdue all harshness and bitterness and abuse, so that truth can find its way through the lives of every one of you. And it will enable you to bear with one another's faults and weaknesses.... So be passionate and faithful in the cause of truth, but also careful and cautious, and be known for your consideration of others, your moderation and restraint. Let it be clear that it is the Lord who works through you, and let honesty and justice be evident in everything you say and in every interaction with other people. Leave no debt outstanding, but

showing forth the work of the Lord, and your honesty and justness in all your words and dealings between man and man; and that you may owe nothing to any man but love, that every one of you may be adorned with a meek and quiet spirit, which is with the Lord of great price.

77 You that come to be vessels of honour and vessels of the mercies of God, have esteem of your bodies, for such as defile their bodies are neither vessels of honour nor vessels of the mercies.

78 Therefore wait... in the measure of the life of God, in it to grow up in love, in virtue and in immortality, in that which doth not fade, which joins and unites your hearts together.

LOVE

79 L iving in the truth ye live in the love and unity.

80 All that worship in the spirit and truth, come to the spirit and truth in their own hearts, and love one another and love enemies.

81 Let the love of God, which is shed abroad in your hearts, cast out all fear.

82 Tender to one another in all convenient outward things, for that is the least love.

83 Make every one's condition in the truth your own; in that you will deny yourselves and become all to all in the truth, so that none may be hurt in the truth, nor made to stumble, nor the blind caused to wander, but be directed into the right way, and all as the tender plants may grow together.

84 For love keeps out of all strife, and is of God; and love and

remember the debt of love you owe to others. Then each of you will be clothed in a humble and quiet spirit, which the Lord values greatly.

77 You who have come to be 'vessels for honourable use,… to which God has shown mercy' (Romans 9:21-23), honour your own bodies, because those who abuse their bodies are neither vessels of honour nor vessels of mercy.

78 Therefore take time… to experience what you have in you of the life of God, and with that experience you will grow in love, in virtue, in that which binds and holds your hearts together, and in that which does not fade away, raising you above death itself.

LOVE

79 Living with reality you find you live with love and you live in unity.

80 All those who worship in the spirit and in truth first come to the spirit and truth in their own hearts, and they love one another and they love their enemies.

81 The love of God has been poured into your hearts, so let it banish all fear.

82 Offer to help one another in practical ways, as need arises, which is a minimal love.

83 Identify with others, whatever their condition spiritually, and in this way you get to deny the claims of your self and become whatever others need you to be for their spiritual welfare (1 Corinthians 9:22). Then no one need get hurt in their spiritual life, or be tripped up, and the blind won't be left to wander, but be guided in the right direction, and all of you, like tender plants, will then grow together.

84 For love avoids strife and love is from God. And selfless love never fails, but keeps the mind detached from things and from strife about

charity never fail, but keep the mind above all outward
things or strife about outward things; and is that which
overcomes evil and casts out all false fear; and it is of God
and unites all the hearts of his people together in the heavenly joy, concord and unity.

85 While I was in Cornwall there were great shipwrecks about
the Land's End. It was the custom of that country at such a
time, both rich and poor went out to get as much of the
wreck as they could, not caring to save the people's lives;
and in some parts of the country they called shipwrecks
God's grace. It grieved my spirit to hear of such unchristian
actions.... Wherefore I was moved to write a paper and
send it to all the parishes.... 'Do not take people's goods
from them by force out of their ships, seamen's or others,
neither covet after them; but rather endeavour to preserve
their lives and goods for them, for that shows a spirit of
compassion, and the spirit of a christian'.

DIFFERENCE

86 If there happen any difference among Friends, either with
Friends or the world, let it be put to reference, if it cannot
be ended between themselves: and all that are concerned to
end any difference, let them have but one ear to one party,
and let them reserve the other ear to hear the other party; so
that they may judge impartially of matters, without affection or favour, or respect of persons.

87 In all matters of business or difference or controversies,
treat one another in such things kindly and gently, and be
not fierce or heady and high minded; for that spirit will
bring men and women to be lovers of themselves and to be
despisers of others and that which is good, which leads
nature out of its course and so loses natural affections, and
at last comes to be without natural affections; which spirit
we see most of christendom is led by: for if they were in

things. And it's love that overcomes evil and banishes fear, that is, fear that's unreal. And love is from God and it holds the hearts of his people together in heavenly joy, harmony and unity.

85 While I was in Cornwall there were great shipwrecks around Land's End. It was the custom in that county at such a time for both rich and poor to go out to get as much of the wreck as they could, without caring to save anyone's life! And in some parts of the county they called shipwrecks 'God's grace'. It grieved my spirit to hear of such unchristian behaviour.... In consequence I was moved to write a paper and send it to all the parishes.... 'Do not take people's goods away from them by force, out of their ships, either the seamen's goods or anyone else's, and don't covet them either. Rather, endeavour to preserve their lives and their goods, for that shows a spirit of compassion, and the spirit of a Christian.'

DIFFERENCE

86 If a difference should arise among Friends, or between Friends and the world, and if it cannot be resolved among themselves, let it be referred to a third party. And all those who are concerned to resolve a difference, let them give only one ear to one party, and reserve the other ear for the other party, so that they can judge matters impartially, without fear or favour, or respect of persons.

87 In all matters of business, difference or controversy, treat one another kindly and gently. Don't be aggressive or head-strong or high-minded, because that attitude only encourages men and women to look after themselves and despise other people, and despise what is good, and it leads them to behave unnaturally so that they lose natural affection, even to the point where they have none left at all. This is the attitude that mostly informs Christian society, as we can see very clearly, for if they had natural affection they would not destroy their fellow humans over matters of religion.

natural affections, they would not destroy their fellow creatures about religion.

FORGIVENESS

88 I came into Wiltshire where we had many precious meetings, though some opposition by one Nathaniel Coleman against the women's meetings at Slaughterford. But as he went out of the house in a rage and passion, he saw the angel of the Lord stand ready with his drawn sword to cut him off. And he came in again, like a dead man, and besought me to pray for him, and said he was a dead man and desired me to forgive him. And I told him if he felt forgiveness from the Lord whom he had opposed, I should freely forgive him.

GROWTH

89 For those with the light... loving it and walking in it and waiting in it, power is given and strength; and being obedient to it and faithful in a little you will grow up to be rulers over much.

90 So every one in your measures of the spirit of God and Christ be faithful, that in it you may increase and answer the Lord in a good life and conversation.

91 Keep your habitations, that ye may every one feel your spring in the light which comes from the Lord, and feel your nourishment and refreshment; which waters the plants and causeth them to grow up in the Lord, from whom the pure, living springs come.

92 In all your meetings be faithful in the power and life, that you may be watered by the spring of life, that you may grow.

93 Ye that have denied the world's fastings, and of their

FORGIVENESS

88 I came into Wiltshire where we had a number of really good meetings, though some opposition too from one Nathaniel Coleman against the women's meetings at Slaughterford. But as he was leaving the house, all in a rage, he saw the angel of the Lord with his sword drawn, ready to cut him down. So he came back in again, looking dead, and begged me to pray for him. He said he was a dead man and wanted me to forgive him. I said to him that if he felt forgiveness from the Lord, whom he had opposed, I would freely forgive him too.

GROWTH

89 To those who love the light and live their lives in it and wait in dependence on it, power is given and strength. And as you obey it and remain faithful to what little you have, you will grow to be responsible for something much bigger.

90 So everyone, if you are faithful to that portion of the spirit of God and Christ that you have each received, you will receive more and you will respond to the Lord by living well and doing well.

91 Look after the place you live in, so that you each become aware of the spring of water emerging in the light from the Lord, and aware of your being nourished and refreshed by it. It is this that waters the plants and makes them grow in the Lord, from whom indeed these pure springs of life all come.

92 As you are faithful in your meeting together, by the power and the life within you, you will be watered by the spring of life itself, and you will grow.

93 You who have rejected fasting as a worldly practice, who refuse to

hanging down their heads like a bulrush for a day, who smite with the fist of wickedness, keep ye the fast of the Lord that breaks the bond of iniquity and lets the oppressed go free, that your health may grow and your light may shine as the morning.

SUMMARY

94 So here in this power of the gospel, all have their liberty and all have unity, and all have liberty in the spirit and unity in the light.

95 Friends everywhere, to the measure of the life of God in you all take heed, that with it your minds may be guided up to the living God from whence light and life come, and virtue and strength and nourishment, so that with the life ye may be kept from that which veils and clouds and darkens, where the mist of darkness cometh over you.... So that in peace, patience, righteousness and temperance and godliness ye may be kept, and all grow up in brotherly kindness, and be kept from that which causeth strife and sects and divisions, so that nothing may rule but the light of God among you.

96 Keep up your meetings for worship, and your men and women's meetings for the affairs of truth, both Monthly and Quarterly. And, after you are settled, you may join together and build a meeting-house. And do not strive about outward things; but dwell in the love of God, for that will unite you together, and make you kind and gentle one towards another; and to seek one another's good and welfare, and to be helpful one to another; and see that nothing be lacking among you, then all will be well. And let temperance and patience and kindness and brotherly love be exercised among you, so that you may abound in virtue, and the true humility; living in peace, showing forth the nature of christianity, that you may all live as a family.

bow your heads like a bulrush for one day while [at other times] you lash out viciously [at those who work for you], make sure you keep the fast of the Lord which is to loose the fetters of injustice and let the oppressed go free. Then you will grow in health and your light will shine like the morning.

SUMMARY

94 So here, with this power of the gospel, all have their liberty and all have unity. They have liberty in the spirit and they have unity in the light.

95 Friends everywhere, take heed to what you all have in you of the life of God, the living God from whom light and life come, and virtue and strength and nourishment. Then with that life you will be kept clear of what tends to veil and cloud and darken your minds, when a mist of darkness comes over you…. You will be kept in a peaceful frame of mind, patient and moderate, able to devote yourself to what is right and sacred. And you will all grow in brotherly and sisterly kindness, free from those feelings that produce strife and division and factions. Then nothing will govern your lives but the light of God within you all.

96 Maintain your meetings for worship, and your men's and women's meetings for the affairs of truth, both monthly and quarterly. And when you are established [as a group] you can get together to build a meeting house. But avoid conflict over material things; rather, inhabit the love of God, for that will unite you, and make you kind and gentle towards one another, willing to seek the good and welfare of one another. It will make you ready to help one another, and to see that every need is met. Then all will be well with you. And see to it that you practise moderation and patience with one another, that you are kind and loving, and then you will overflow with virtue and with true humility, living in peace, showing in your lives what Christianity really is, so that you can all live together as a family.

ENDNOTES for part two

1. 'To all who love the Lord Jesus Christ' (1654), in Doctrinals, Works 4:43.
2. Epistle 186 (1659), Works 7:175.
3. Epistle 4 (1651), Works 7:18f.
4. Epistle 132 (1656), Works 7:130. Cf. 2 Corinthians 3:1-3.
5. Epistle 24 (1653), Works 7:31.
6. Epistle 35 (1653), Works 7:42.
7. Epistle 130 (1656), Works 7:124.
8. Epistle 249 (1667), Works 7:298. The quotation is from Matthew 18:20.
9. Epistle 131 (1656), Works 7:127. On 'the beast, false prophet' see Revelation 16:13; 19:19f., on 'the antichrist' see Glossary. The 'true church' is being compared to the people of Israel who were led through 'the wilderness' for forty years to test them; cf. e.g. Deuteronomy 8:2.
10. Journal (for 1651), ed. Ellwood, in Works 1:128.
11. Epistle 308 (1674), Works 8:61.
12. Epistle 373 (to Friends in Jamaica, 1681), Works 8:210.
13. Epistle 420 ('to Friends, captives at Macqueness', 1690, which was Fox's last letter), Works 8:311.
14. Epistle 222 (1662), Works 7:229. Cf. 1 Peter 3:4.
15. An epistle to Friends of 1658, Journal, ed. Nickalls, pp.340f. Cf. ed. Ellwood for fuller text, in Works 1:366f.
16. Epistle 145 (1657), Works 7:138.

17. Epistle 181 (1659), *Works* 7:171.
18. A paper of 1654, in *Doctrinals*, *Works* 4:43.
19. Epistle 217 (1662), *Works* 7:219f.
20. Epistle 109 (1655), *Works* 7:109.
21. *Journal* (for 1648), ed. Ellwood, in *Works* 1:85.
22. Epistle 313 (1674), *Works* 8:70.
23. Epistle 313 (1674), *Works* 8:71. The quotation is from 1 Corinthians 14:40.
24. Epistle 361 (1679), *Works* 8:183.
25. Epistle 317 (1675), *Works* 8:83.
26. Epistle 284 (1671), *Works* 8:33.
27. *Journal* (for 1667), ed. Nickalls, p.514. Cf. 2 Timothy 1:10.
28. Epistle 291 ('to all the women's meetings', 1672), *Works* 8:40.
29. *Journal* (for 1668), ed. Nickalls, p.524.
30. Epistle 320 ('An encouragement to all the faithful women's meetings in the world, who assemble together in the fear of God for the service of truth', 1676), *Works* 8:96.
31. Epistle 320 (as above, 1676), *Works* 8:95.
32. Epistle 320 (as above, 1676), *Works* 8:97. Cf. 1 Peter 3:7; 4:10.
33. Epistle 313 (1674), *Works* 8:69f. The quotations are from 1 Corinthians 11:8,12.
34. 'The Women Learning in Silence, or the Mystery of the Woman's Subjection to her Husband' (1656), in *Doctrinals*, *Works* 4:109.
35. An epistle to Friends of 1657, in *Journal*, ed. Ellwood, in *Works* 1:345f. Cf. Acts 2:17 (re. Joel 2:28); Acts 2:4; 1 Peter 4:10. The quotation about fruit may be from Romans 7:4.
36. An epistle to Friends 'who had received a part of the ministry, concerning the exercise of their spiritual gifts in the church' (1658), in *Journal*, ed. Ellwood, in *Works* 1:367. See Glossary on 'settle'.
37. An epistle to Friends of 1658, in *Journal*, ed. Ellwood, in *Works* 1:370.

38. 'To all that would know the way to the kingdom' (1653), in *Doctrinals*, *Works* 4:19. On 'the unquenchable fire' see Matthew 3:12; Luke 3:17.

39. Epistle 12 (1652), *Works* 7:21. Cf. 1 Timothy 4:2.

40. Epistle 222 (1662), *Works* 7:237. Cf. John 10:12f.

41. 'A word from the Lord to all the world' (1654), in *Doctrinals*, *Works* 4:34.

42. Epistle 281 (1670), *Works* 8:31.

43. Epistle 130 (1656), *Works* 7:122.

44. *Journal* (for 1674), ed. Nickalls, p.687.

45. *Journal* (for 1652), ed. Nickalls, p.136.

46. *Journal* (for 1657), ed. Nickalls, p.292.

47. *Journal* (for 1648), ed. Ellwood, in *Works* 1:88f.

48. *Journal* (for 1648), ed. Ellwood, in *Works* 1:90.

49. *Journal* (for 1652), ed. Ellwood, in *Works* 1:140.

50. *Journal* (for 1668), ed. Nickalls, p.520.

51. Epistle 238 (1664), *Works* 7:259.

52. Epistle 40 (1653), *Works* 7:49.

53. Epistle 221 (1662), *Works* 7:223f. On 'laying hand on no man' see 1 Timothy 5:22.

54. Epistle 5 ('To his parents', 1652), *Works* 7:19. Cf. John 10:5 on 'the voice of the stranger'.

55. Epistle 367 (1682), *Works* 8:196.

56. *Journal* (for 1653), ed. Nickalls, p.170.

57. *Journal* (for 1658), ed. Ellwood, in *Works* 1:371.

58. Epistle 288 (1671), *Works* 8:38.

59. Epistle 130 (1656), *Works* 7:122.

60. Epistle 311 (1674), *Works* 8:63.

61. Epistle 245 (1666), *Works* 7:275f. Cf. John 8:32; 4:24.

62. Epistle 200 ('on justice', 1661), *Works* 7:193.

63. Epistle 235 (1664), *Works* 7:257.

64. Epistle 371 (1681), *Works* 8:201.

65. *Journal* (for 1658), ed. Ellwood, in *Works* 1:378.

66. Epistle 48 (1653), *Works* 7:63. Cf. Ephesians 5:8,15.
67. Epistle 104 (1655), *Works* 7:105.
68. Epistle 79 (1654), *Works* 7:88.
69. Epistle 185 (1659), *Works* 7:174f.
70. Epistle 296 (1673), *Works* 8:45.
71. Epistle 353 (1678), *Works* 8:155.
72. Epistle 41 (1653), *Works* 7:49.
73. Epistle 58 (1654), *Works* 7:73.
74. Epistle 244 (1666), *Works* 7:274. See Glossary on 'naked'.
75. *Journal*, ed. Nickalls, pp.400f. This is from the Peace Declaration of 1660 which Fox wrote with a number of other Friends. On 'fables' see 2 Peter 1:16; on 'praise of them that do well' 1 Peter 2:13,14.
76. Epistle 364 (1680), *Works* 8:190f. Cf. Philippians 2:3,4; 4:5; Romans 12:10; 13:8.
77. Epistle 244 (1666), *Works* 7:274. Cf. Romans 9:21-23; 2 Timothy 2:20f.
78. Epistle 77 (1654), *Works* 7:87.
79. Epistle 142 (1657), *Works* 7:136.
80. Epistle 260 (1668), *Works* 7:317.
81. Epistle 352 (1678), *Works* 8:152. Cf. Romans 5:5; 1 John 4:18.
82. Epistle 215 (1661), *Works* 7:215. See Glossary on 'tender' and contrast with use in the next extract, 2:83.
83. Epistle 384 (1683), *Works* 8:232.
84. Epistle 417 (1689), *Works* 8:308. Cf. 1 Corinthians 13:8; 1 John 4:18.
85. *Journal* (for 1659), ed. Ellwood, in *Works* 1:394f.
86. Epistle 360 (1679), *Works* 8:173.
87. Epistle 383 (1683), *Works* 8:230.
88. A paper of 1673, in *Journal*, ed. Nickalls, pp.666f.
89. *This is to all people who stumble at God's commands* (1660), a tract not since published. Cf. Matthew 25:23; Luke 19:17,26.
90. Epistle 288 (1671), *Works* 8:37. Cf. Ephesians 4:11-16 and see

Glossary on 'measure'.

91. Epistle 155 (1657), *Works* 7:147f.
92. Epistle 281 (1670), *Works* 8:31.
93. Epistle 167 (1658), *Works* 7:156. Cf. Isaiah 58:3-8.
94. Epistle 318 (1675), *Works* 8:80.
95. Epistle 63 (1654), *Works* 7:76.
96. Epistle 340 (1676), *Works* 8:131.

ANTHOLOGY
part 3: *the world*

CREATION

1   Now was I come up in the spirit through the flaming sword into the paradise of God. All things were new, and all the creation gave another smell unto me than before, beyond what words can utter. I knew nothing but pureness and innocency and righteousness, being renewed up into the image of God by Christ Jesus, so that I say I was come up to the state of Adam which he was in before he fell. The creation was opened to me.... Great things did the Lord lead me into and wonderful depths were opened to me, beyond what can by words be declared; but as people come into subjection to the spirit of God and grow up in the image and power of the Almighty, they may receive the word of wisdom that opens all things, and come to know the hidden unity in the eternal being.

2   He that believes in the light sees the joy, the comfort, the paradise, the garden of God, the garden of pleasure. He sees how they walk under curtains, how God has garnished the heavens and clothed the earth with grass and trees and herbs, how all the creatures stand in their places, keeping their unity. He sees the sun and moon in their courses, and the stars keeping the law of the covenant of God.

3   So ye in the power of the Lord God... see over that which brought destruction, in which power... life and immortality come to light and captivate that which hid life and immortality.... In which power of God... which goes over the power of darkness and was before it was, ye see before all transgression, and how all things were blessed.

4   Therefore ye all dearly beloved Friends, that know the universal power of God that goes over all the apostasy and the fall (where the curse and wrath and woe are), to the beginning where all things are blest to you that live in love and life.

CREATION

1 I now came up in the spirit past the flaming sword into the paradise of God. Everything was new. And the whole creation gave off another smell to what I knew before, beyond what I could ever express in words. I knew nothing but purity and innocence and rightness as I was renewed in the image of God by Christ Jesus, so that, as I say, I entered the state that Adam was in before he fell. The creation was opened up to me.... Great things I was led to [see] by the Lord and wonderful depths were revealed to me, beyond what I could ever put in words. But as people surrender to the spirit of God and grow in the image and power of the Almighty, they too can receive the word of wisdom that opens up everything, and they too can come to know the hidden unity in the eternal being.

2 Whoever believes in the light comes to see the joy, the comfort, the paradise, the garden of God, the garden of pleasure. They see how they 'walk under curtains', how God has 'garnished the heavens' and clothed the earth with grass and trees and herbs, how every creature occupies the space given to it so that together they can maintain their unity. They see the sun and moon following the course set for them, and the stars keeping the law of God's covenant [with creation].

3 So, with the power of the Lord God, ... you can look beyond what has been destructive. For with this power we have become aware of life and of what transcends death, and how they have taken captive the very thing that kept them from view.... And with this power of God... which overcomes the power of darkness, as it preceded it in time, you must look beyond all that has gone wrong to the time when everything was blessed.

4 Therefore all you dearly loved Friends, [you] know the universal power of God that goes back behind the history of betrayal and alienation – where the misery and guilt and unhappiness come from – to the very beginning where everything is blessed to you who live in love and life.

5 The word of the Lord to all Friends, who... have received wisdom from God, that with it ye may come to know how to order the creation with the wisdom by which all things were made.

6 Wait all in the light for the wisdom by which all things were made, with it to use all the Lord's creatures to his glory... for which end they were created, and with the wisdom by which they were made ye may be kept out of the misuse of them, in the image of God, that ye may come to see that the 'earth is the Lord's and the fulness thereof'.

7 Let not the lust go out to anything which is mortal, to be servants thereto, but mind the joining to the life. Here ye are kept in the image of God. Not but that ye may use the creatures lawfully, but being kept in the image of God, ye are kept as kings over all the creatures and over the creation; here ye will see all things, and by whom they stand.

WORLD

8 So, live in the truth by which ye may see over that which stains, corrupts, cankers, loads and burdens the creation.

9 This light which is of God lets thee see all the works of the world, and draws thee out of the worships of the world, and keeps thee in the fear of God.

10 All Friends that speak abroad, see that it be in the life of God.... In that wait to receive power... whereby you may come to feel the light which comprehends time and the world and fathoms it, which believed in gives you the victory over the world.

11 All my dear brethren, babes of God, born of the immortal seed, whose dwelling is in the power that upholds all things, which power is made manifest, which hath brought

5 A word from the Lord to all Friends who… have received wisdom from God: may you learn how to handle the creation with the very wisdom by which it was all made.

6 Wait in the light, all of you, for the wisdom with which everything was made, so that you can use everything the Lord has made for his glory, which was the whole purpose of their having been made. Then, deploying that very wisdom, you will not be led to misuse them but learn to live 'in the image of God' (Genesis 1:27) and to see that 'the earth is the Lord's and everything in it' (Psalm 24:1).

7 Beware of a lust for anything mortal, because you only become slaves to it, but rather connect with the life [inside you]. Here you are kept in your likeness to God. Not that you should avoid using things in ways allowed by the law [of God], but as you are kept in God's likeness, you are called to exercise responsibility over everything God has made. And from here you will be able to see everything, and by whom everything exists.

WORLD

8 So live by the truth which will give you a view of creation beyond what spoils, corrupts, poisons, overloads and burdens it.

9 This light which comes from God enables you to see what the world is doing, and it draws you away from the world's religious practices, and it keeps you in an attitude of reverence for God.

10 All you Friends who go out speaking, see that it's grounded in the life of God.… Wait in that life until you receive the power… which will make you aware of the light, because that light is capable of grasping the world and the transience of everything in it, and it can fathom its depths. And when you trust that light it will give you victory over whatever in the world may threaten you.

11 All my dear brothers and sisters, God's babies, born from a seed that cannot die, [you are] living in the power that upholds everything, the

you to him that was in the beginning, before the world was, and with the life to comprehend the world, and that which is in it, and what it is, and what it lies in.

12 Stir abroad whilst the door is open and the light shineth; and so go on in that which letteth you see the world, to comprehend it and to see what is imprisoned by it and suffereth by it. So the Lord give you an understanding in all things.

13 All dwell in the power and spirit of God, with which ye will comprehend all that which is to change, with that which doth not change and hath no end.

THAT OF GOD

14 Examine and search with that which is eternal, which speaks to that which is in prison in others. And ye that are led forth to exhort, or to reprove, do it with all diligence, taking all opportunities, reproving that which devours the creation and thereby destroys the very human reason. For the truth doth preserve everything in its place.

15 There is something of the invisible power of God in every man and woman.

16 Christ enlightens every man that cometh into the world, that everyone may believe in the light and may become a child of the light, and have eternal life.... And as you do walk in the light, grace, spirit and gospel you may turn others to it. That you may have unity with them in it, and that they may come out of the spiritual prison of death.

17 So, according to the light of Christ in them all, speak, that to it their minds may be guided; and declare the truth to them, which is agreeable to that of God in every one's conscience.

power which has now been revealed, which brought you to the one
who has been there from the beginning, in fact from before the world
began, and with that life has enabled you to understand the world, and
what's in it, and what it is, and what makes it what it is.

12 Get out there while the door is still open and the light still shines. And
continue to rely on that [inner] capacity to see the world, to understand it and to see what is held captive by it and made to suffer by it.
So may the Lord give you understanding in every situation.

13 If you all stay with the power and spirit of God, you will be able to
understand what is bound to change, and be able to distinguish it from
what doesn't change, or come to an end.

THAT OF GOD

14 Examine and search with that resource in you which is eternal, which
speaks to that part in others which is imprisoned. And those of you who
have been led to go out and encourage others, or to confront them, do
it diligently, taking every opportunity, confronting that especially which
devours creation, and in that way destroys human reason itself. Truth,
on the other hand, preserves everything in relation to the whole.

15 There is something of the invisible power of God in every man and
woman.

16 Christ enlightens everyone who comes into the world, so that everyone may believe in the light and become a child of the light, and have
eternal life.... And as you live your life in the light – in grace, in the
spirit and in the gospel – you will be able to turn others to it. You will
then have unity with them in the light, and they will be free to leave
the spiritual prison of death.

17 So speak to them according to the light of Christ which is in them all,
so that their minds might be guided towards it. And declare to them
the truth which agrees with what they all already have of God within
their own consciences.

18 Go on in the truth, answering it in every one in the inward parts.

19 Be wise and low, and take heed of abusing the power of God, but live in it, in the still life, patient, to the answering the good in all, to the refreshing one of another and not to the stumbling.

20 And so, living in the light and truth ye may answer the light and truth in every man and woman.

21 Love gathereth into love.

22 Sound deep to the witness of God in every man.

23 Our desire is… that you may answer the truth of God in all people with the word of life, and also answer the good in all with a godly and a holy life and conversation.

WITNESS OF WORDS

24 If you would have them come to the knowledge of truth, let them know it, and where it is to be found.

25 If any be moved to go to the steeple-houses or markets, or to reprove sin in the gate, or to exhort high or low, or to reprove them, reason not with flesh and blood, nor quench the spirit. And when ye have done, in the same spirit live, and then ye will have peace and rest, and fellowship with God and one with another.

26 And set up truth, and confound deceit which stains the earth and cumbers the ground. The dead stinks upon the earth and with it the earth is stained, therefore bury it…. And go on in the work of the Lord, that ye may trample upon all deceit within and without.

18 Continue in the truth, responding to it as it exists in everyone's inner being.

19 Be wise and humble, careful not to abuse the power of God, but live in the power, in the life of stillness, and be patient. And do all this so as to [cor]respond to the good in everyone, and to be a source of refreshment to one another rather than a cause of trouble.

20 And so, living in the light and truth you will be able to respond to the light and truth in every man and woman.

21 Love gathers into love.

22 Make deep soundings to the witness of God in everyone.

23 Our desire is… that you will be able to respond to the truth of God in everyone with the word of life, and also to respond to the good in everyone with a life obviously devoted to God and the sacred.

WITNESS OF WORDS

24 If you want them to come to know truth, let them know this, and where truth is to be found.

25 If any of you are moved to visit the steeple-houses or markets, or to confront people publicly about wrongdoing, or to encourage people of whatever class, or to confront them, don't appeal to their merely human reason and don't stifle the spirit. And when you have finished, live in the same spirit in which you spoke, and you will then have peace and rest, and fellowship with God and with one another.

26 And establish truth and overthrow deceit, which pollutes the earth and obstructs the way. The dead lie foul on the earth and with them the earth is polluted, so bury them.… And go on with the Lord's work to trample on all deceit, both in you yourselves and in other people.

27 Be bold in the power of truth, and valiant for it upon the earth, treading, triumphing over and trampling all deceit under foot, inward and outward; having done it in yourselves in particular, ye have power over the world in general.... And being written all in one another's hearts, have all one voice and the pure language of truth, where in all plainness of speech things may be spoken in nakedness of heart one unto another in the eternal unity in the one spirit.

28 Friends of God and brethren, this is a warning to you all from the Lord God and Jesus Christ, that all that ye speak it may be in plainness of speech, according to that of God in all consciences, and that it may proceed from that of God in you, the light of Christ, that all your words be words of life to the life, and death to the death where it reigns above the light. And that all words which are spoken be in plainness of speech, that the light of Christ in all consciences, which he hath enlightened every one withal, may witness your words to be the words of life, so that dwelling in the light, to that of God ye may be made manifest in all consciences, which shall be their condemnation that hate it. Ye that dwell in the light and walk in the light use plainness of speech and plain words, single words in the single life, pure words from the pure life, seasoned words seasoned with grace.

29 Nor to the world speak confusedly, to speak the plural for the singular, and when ye are among the world speak as the world doth, and when ye are amongst Friends speak as they do: this spirit is not from the spirit of God, but is hypocrisy and for judgment. And so let the truth have its passage in all things, and speak true words and not false, with the light ye will see; who act contrary to it will be condemned by it. So let Friends be distinct from all the world in their language.

30 Let your patience be perfect, and all your words seasoned with grace, that they may edify; by which ye may season

27 Be bold in the power that truth gives you, and be valiant for truth on the earth, treading down and triumphing over and trampling all deceit under foot, in yourselves and in others. And having done that in yourselves in particular you will have power over the world in general.... And since you are all written in one another's hearts, see that you all speak with one voice and in the pure language of truth. For there, in the plainness of speech, things can be said in complete openness of heart to one another, with the eternal unity of the one spirit.

28 Friends of God, brothers and sisters, here is a plea to you all from the Lord God and from Jesus Christ: be sure that everything you say is said plainly, according to what you have of God in your consciences, and be sure that it proceeds from that source, the light of Christ, so that your words may be words of life, evoking life [in others], or indeed [words of] death to death [in others] where that rules over the light. And be sure that the words you speak are all spoken plainly so that the light of Christ in everyone's conscience, the light with which he has enlightened everyone, will recognise your words to be words of life. Then insofar as you live in the light, you will be revealed to that something in the conscience of other people that comes from God – which, if they reject it, will make them know they are in the wrong. So you who live your lives in the light use plainness of speech and plain words, honest words in an honest life, pure words from the pure life, seasoned words 'seasoned with grace' (Colossians 4:6).

29 Don't confuse people in the way you speak either, using the plural when you mean the singular, for example, or speaking as the world does when you're out in the world but speaking as Friends do when you're with them. This way of being is not inspired by God, but is hypocritical and should be condemned. So let the truth have its way in everything you do. Let your words be true and not false, as the light will show you – and those who disregard the light will be made aware by the light how wrong they are. So let Friends be distinct in their language from the rest of the world.

30 Be as patient as you need to be, and let everything you say be

the earth, your hearts being established in the same, over all the unsavoury words and talkers, and live in the truth above them.

31 Dwell in the light which lets you see the evil communication, and with the light give judgment upon it in the particular and first judge it there.... So all walk in the light with which ye are enlightened, for it will teach you all... pure communication.

WITNESS OF LIFE

32 This is to you all that are in the light... that they that act contrary to the light and believe not in it, who know not the word and will not be won with the word (speaking to them), that your chaste conversation (ye walking in the light which comes from the word) may answer to the light in them, which they hate and walk contrary to; that your chaste conversation may judge them and ye may win them.

33 Keep out of the many words of the world, and take heed of a liberty of going into them, but keep in the power of the Lord God... that your lives and conversations may preach to all men, and adorn the truth of God, and speak in the hearts of all men.

34 Let your moderation be known unto all men, honouring all men, that is, having them all in esteem, that ye may set them in the way of salvation and life. That the power of God may come over them, that your meekness and gentleness may prevail over the rough.

35 Postscript: 'Honouring all men' is reaching that of God in every man, for that brings to seek the honour of God; the other fades, and reacheth not to that of God in man; for the saints which were to honour all men were in that of

seasoned with grace, so that it edifies people. And by speaking this way you will season the earth, your own hearts being established in the process, and you will be free from unsavoury ways of speaking, and unsavoury speakers, and you will live in the truth beyond their reach.

31 Stay with the light when it shows you that communication is bad, and declare it to be bad precisely as the light shows you in that particular instance, and let your judgment begin with that instance.... So all of you live your lives in the light which has enlightened you, for this will teach you all... pure communication.

WITNESS OF LIFE

32 Here's something for all of you who live in the light:... when people act contrary to the light and don't believe in it, when they know nothing of the word and won't be won over by the word, i.e. your speaking to them, then it's down to your pure way of life, i.e. your acting according to the light that comes from the word, to evoke the light in them, which they themselves have rejected and refused to follow. Your pure way of life might then show them what they are doing and win them over.

33 Avoid those endless discussions that people generally get into. Don't allow yourselves the indulgence of getting involved. But stay with the power of the Lord God... so that your lives and actions will communicate to people and resonate in their hearts and your lives will give expression to the beauty of God's truth.

34 Let your moderation be evident to everyone, and 'honour all people', that is, hold them all in esteem so that you can point them in the direction of liberation and life. Then the power of God might take hold of them, and your humility and gentleness might prevail over their roughness.

35 Postscript: 'honour all people' (1 Peter 2:17) is in effect to reach that part of everyone that comes from God, for it encourages them to look for God's honour. Not to honour people is to fail to reach that divine part of their humanity. For the saints who were called to 'honour all

God which reached to that of God in all men.

36 Do rightly, justly, truly, holy, equally to all people in all
things, and that is according to that of God in every man,
and the witness of God and the wisdom of God and the
life of God in yourselves; and there ye are serviceable in
your generation, labouring in the thing that is good, which
doth not spoil nor destroy nor waste the creation upon
lusts.... In the fear of God serve him, and be diligent and
not stubborn in any thing, but pliable in the power of God
that keeps you over all the powers of unrighteousness,
acting so in that, that ye may be a good savour in all
nations, islands and places where ye come in the hearts of
all people, doing truly and plainly, uprightly, faithfully,
justly and honestly, according to the light of Christ Jesus in
every man, that ye may witness to all. Then will your
words, lives and conversations preach and manifest that ye
serve God in the new life.... Loathe deceit and all unrighteousness, hard-heartedness, wronging, cozening, cheating
or unjust dealing, but live and reign in the righteous life and
power of God, and wisdom... and to answer the good and
just principle in all people, and that will win people to deal
with you, 'doing truth to all, without respect to persons', to
high or low whatsoever, young or old, rich or poor. And
so here your lives and words will preach wherever ye
come.... So let your lives preach, let your light shine....
And let all your actions and words be one with the witness
of God in all people. Amen.

37 Be patterns, be examples in all countries, places, islands,
nations, wherever you come, that your carriage and life
may preach among all sorts of people, and to them. Then
you will come to walk cheerfully over the world, answering that of God in every one, whereby in them ye may be a
blessing and make the witness of God in them to bless you.

people' were themselves living from that divine source which was
reaching out to that source in everyone else.

36 Act rightly, justly, truly, purely towards everyone you meet and in
every situation, with equal regard for all, and that means act according to what everyone has of God within them, and also according to
that witness of God, wisdom of God and life of God you have within
yourselves. That way you will be serviceable in your generation, spend-
ing your effort on something worthwhile, something which doesn't
spoil or destroy or waste the creation on selfish desire.... Serve God
in an attitude of reverence towards him, and be diligent in what you
do rather than stubbornly resisting your task. Be pliable in your dependence on God's power, which keeps you free from the powers of
wrongdoing, and in so doing you should become a good savour in
people's hearts in every nation, island or place where you go. Act truly
and plainly, faithfully, justly, honestly, and with integrity, according to
the light of Christ Jesus in everyone, so that you can bear witness to all.
Then it will be evident to everyone from your words and lives and
actions that you're working for God, from an experience of the new
life.... Loathe deceit and every kind of injustice: hard-heartedness,
betrayal, fraud, cheating and unfair dealing. But live with freedom in
the life and power of God which will enable you to do the right thing
and to act wisely... responding to the good and just source of life in
everyone, and that will win people over to deal with you. Act according to truth in relation to everyone you meet, high or low, young or
old, rich or poor. So in this way your lives and words will communicate wherever you go.... So let your lives communicate, let your light
shine.... And let all your actions and words be harmonious with the
witness of God in all people. Amen.

37 Be models, be examples in every country, place, island or nation that
you visit, so that your bearing and life might communicate with all
sorts of people, and to them. Then you'll happily walk across the world
to evoke that something of God in everybody, with the result that they
come to see you as a blessing in their lives, and you receive a blessing
from God's witness in them.

TESTIMONIES

38 Be faithful in your testimonies of life and light, against all those things which have come up in this night of apostasy from the light, life and power of God.

39 Keep your testimony against the world's vain ways, words, fashions, customs and worships, as you did at first.

40 As for the customs and fashions of the world, bowing and making obeisance with cap and knee, which men and women have done one to another, which lived without the fear of the Lord, we deny; but we honour all men in the Lord with our souls and with our hearts, and who looks for these things outwardly there is a fleshly principle, for these things may be done and are practised and the heart full of envy; therefore all these fashions we deny.

41 An exhortation to keep to the ancient principles of truth:
Friends, keep at a word in all your dealings without oppression.
And keep to the sound language, thou to every one.
And keep your testimony against the world's vain fashions.
And keep your testimony against the hireling priests, and their tithes and maintenance.
And against the old mass-houses, and the repairing of them.
And against the priests' and the world's joining in marriages.
And your testimony against swearing and the world's corrupt manners.
And against all looseness, pleasures and profaneness whatsoever.
And against all the world's evil ways, vain worships and religions, and to stand up for God's.

TESTIMONIES

38 Be faithful in maintaining your protests of life and light against all those things that have arisen during the night, when people had fallen away from the light, life and power of God.

39 Keep up your protest against the emptiness of the way the world lives, speaks, socialises, dresses and worships, just as you did at the beginning.

40 When it comes to the way people dress and socialise in the world, bowing and scraping to one another as men and women do, without any reverence for the Lord in their lives – we'll have nothing to do with it. On the other hand we respect every human being with our heart and soul, out of regard for the Lord. And when people look for respect in external behaviour we can see a purely human attitude at work there, for they can do these things, and do do these things, while their hearts are full of envy. So we'll have nothing to do with all these fashions.

41 A word of encouragement to maintain the old principles of truth:
Friends, speak briefly in all your dealings, without oppressing anyone.
And keep to the sound use of language, 'thou' to every single person.
And keep up your protest against the emptiness of the world's fashionable behaviour.
And keep up your protest against the practice of giving priests a salary for their work and charging their costs to the people.
And against the old 'mass houses' [churches], and the repairing of them.
And against the priests and the world 'marrying' people.
And your protest against swearing on oath, and [other forms of] corrupt behaviour.
And against every kind of moral looseness, pleasure-seeking and profanity.
And against all the bad ways and empty worship and religion of the world – and stand up for God's.

PEACE

42 Our principle is, and our practices have always been, to seek peace and ensue it and to follow after righteousness and the knowledge of God, seeking the good and welfare and doing that which tends to the peace of all. We know that wars and fightings proceed from the lusts of men (as Jas.iv.1-3), out of which lusts the Lord hath redeemed us, and so out of the occasion of war. The occasion of which war, and war itself (wherein envious men, who are lovers of themselves more than lovers of God, lust, kill and desire to have men's lives or estates) ariseth from the lust. All bloody principles and practices, we, as to our own particulars, do utterly deny, with all outward wars and strife and fightings with outward weapons, for any end or under any pretence whatsoever. And this is our testimony to the whole world.... We whom the Lord hath called into the obedience of his truth have denied wars and fightings and cannot again any more learn it. This is a certain testimony unto all the world of the truth of our hearts in this particular, that as God persuadeth every man's heart to believe, so they may receive it.

43 The time of my commitment to the house of correction being very near out, and there being many new soldiers raised, the commissioners would have made me captain over them; and the soldiers cried, they would have none but me. So the keeper of the house of correction was commanded to bring me before the commissioners and soldiers in the market place, where they offered me that preferment, as they called it, asking me if I would not take up arms for the commonwealth against Charles Stuart? I told them I knew from whence all wars arose, even from the lusts, according to James's doctrine, and that I lived in the virtue of that life and power that took away the occasion of all wars.

44 The postures of war I never learned; my weapons are spiritual,

PEACE

42 Our principle is what we have always in fact practised: to seek for peace and to follow what is right and conducive to knowing God, seeking the good and welfare of all and doing what makes for peace between them. We know that fighting and war proceed from human passions – James 4:1-3 – passions from which the Lord has delivered us. So he has delivered us from the cause of war itself. The cause of war, and war itself – in which envious people, who love themselves more than God, lust after people's lives or property and [therefore] kill for it – arise from this passion. So we utterly reject all principles and practices of violence – in our own lives, that is – along with all physical war and strife, all fighting with material weapons, for any purpose or under any pretence whatever. And this is our solemn declaration to the whole world.... We have rejected fighting and war because the Lord has called us to obey his truth, so we cannot now take them up again. This is a confident declaration to the whole world of the truth of our hearts in this case, in the hope that they receive it as God persuades everyone's heart to accept it.

43 My time in the house of correction was very nearly up, and at the same time many new soldiers were being recruited for the army, so the commissioners decided they wanted me for their captain – and the soldiers insisted they would have nobody else. The keeper of the house of correction was commanded to bring me before the commissioners and the soldiers in the market place, where they offered me the 'preferment', as they called it, inviting me to take up arms for the Commonwealth against Charles Stuart. But I told them that I knew where wars came from, namely 'the passions', as James had taught (James 4:1-3), and that I lived by the strength of that life and power that took away the cause of all war.

44 The arts of war I never did learn. My weapons are spiritual, not physical, because I don't need physical weapons to fight. I am a follower of the one who said, 'My kingdom is not of this world'.

and not carnal, for with carnal weapons I do not fight. I am a follower of him who said, 'My kingdom is not of this world'.

45 Christ's church was never established by blood, nor held up by prisons: neither was the foundation of it laid by carnal, weaponed men, nor is it preserved by such. But when men went from the spirit and truth, then they took up carnal weapons to maintain their outward forms, and yet cannot preserve them with their carnal weapons, for one plucketh down another's form with his outward weapons. And this work and doing hath been among the Christians in name since they lost the spirit.

46 We are not against any man, but desire that the blessing of the Lord may come upon all men, and that which brings the curse may be destroyed; and in patience do we wait for that, and with spiritual weapons against it do we wrestle, and not against any man or woman's person.

47 Where the mind is stayed upon the Lord, there is a perfect peace, for it is a whole peace, which cannot be broken.... All imperfect peace may be broken, that is when the mind is stayed upon the creature or in any creature, and not upon the Creator; or in any outward things, goods, houses, lands or inventions of vanities, in the foolish vain fashions, which the lust of the eye and the pride of life go into, which will defile and corrupt it. When any of these things fail and are not according to your mind, it being in them, then your peace is broken, and you are cross and brittle and envy gets up.... The apostle said to the saints, 'that he had learned in all conditions to be content'. (Mark) in all conditions.

JUSTICE

48 Live in the life of truth and let the truth speak in all things, and righteousness; and let justice be acted and holiness in all things, without any guile, fraud or deceit....

45 Christ's church wasn't established by blood, nor was it sustained by prisons. Its foundation wasn't laid by soldiers, and it isn't preserved by them either. But when people abandoned the spirit and truth, they then took up physical weapons to maintain the external structures [they had put in the place of spirit], but even then they haven't been able to preserve them with physical weapons because one or other of them is always using their weapons to pull down someone else's structure! And this is what the so-called Christians have been doing ever since they lost the spirit.

46 We are not opposed to anyone. We only desire that everyone may experience the blessing of the Lord, and that what brings misery to their lives may be brought to an end. We wait with patience for that to happen, and we fight for it too, with spiritual weapons, but we don't fight against anyone's person, whether a woman or a man.

47 Where the mind rests on the Lord, there is perfect peace – perfect because it is whole, unbreakable… An imperfect peace can be broken, that is, when the mind rests on or in someone or something that is created, and not on the creator himself, or when it rests on external things, on consumer goods, houses, property or new objects of pride, on foolish, empty fashions which the eye can easily be drawn to by pride and desire, and thereby be degraded and corrupted. When any of these things fail you and come to displease you, because you are attached to them your peace is broken, and you are then angry and insecure, and envy creeps in… The apostle said to the saints that he had learned to be content whatever his situation (Philippians 4:11). Note that: whatever his situation.

JUSTICE

48 Live your life on the basis of truth and let truth have its say in everything, and let what is right be heard too. Let what is just and holy be acted on, without any guile, fraud or deceit… In whatever work you do for a living speak the truth, act on the truth, do what is just and right in all your actions, in all your practices, in all your words, in all

In all husbandry speak truth, act truth, doing justly and
uprightly in all your actions; in all your practices, in all
your words, in all your dealings, buyings, sellings, changings and commerce with people, let truth be the head and
practise it.... And this is more than all the talkers of justice,
righteousness and holiness, whose life denies what their
tongues profess and talk of.... In the power of God and his
life, in which ye have justice, ye have truth, ye have equity,
ye have righteousness, and it cometh to be to you as natural.

49 O ye earthly-minded men, give over oppressing the poor;
exalt not yourselves above your fellow-creatures, for ye are
all of one mould and blood; you that set your nests on high,
join house to house, field to field, till there be no place for
the poor, woe is your portion. The earth is the Lord's and
the fulness thereof. And you that have not so much of the
earth, give over your murmuring and reasoning, fretting
and grudging, for all your want is the want of God; the
righteous God is coming to give to every one of you
according to your works.

50 God's hand is turned against you all that have destroyed
God's creatures upon your lust, that have wronged by
unjust dealing, and defrauded, and have oppressed and have
respected the persons of the proud, and such as be in gay
apparel, and lend not your ear to the cry of the poor.

51 Let all those abbey lands, glebe lands that are given to the
priests be given to the poor of the nation, and let all the
great houses, abbeys, steeple houses and White Hall be for
alms houses (or some other use than what they are) for all
the blind and lame to be there, and not to go begging up
and down the streets.... Let all these fines that belong to the
lords of manors be given to the poor people, for the lords
have enough.... Let all the poor people, blind and lame and
cripples be provided for in the nation, that there might not
be a beggar in England nor England's dominions.

your buying, selling, exchanging and commercial dealings with people. Let truth be your first concern and put it into practice.... You have to do more than those people who talk about justice, rightness and holiness while their lives deny what they talk about and profess to believe in... Living in this power and life of God in which you have justice, you also have truth and equity and rightness, and these things become quite natural for you.

49 Oh you materially minded people, stop oppressing the poor. Don't elevate yourselves above your fellow human beings, for you all come from the same mould, the same blood. You that build your nests up high, add house to house, field to field, till there is nowhere left for the poor, you will surely come to grief. 'The earth is the Lord's and everything in it' (Psalm 24:1). And you that don't have so much of the earth, stop grumbling and arguing, fretting and fuming, for what you are really missing in all this is God. And the God who is fair and just is surely coming to reward you according to what you have done.

50 God's hand is turned against all you who, in pursuit of your lusts, have destroyed what he has made, who have wronged people in unfair dealing, and have defrauded and oppressed them, while you favour people who think they are superior, who dress in fine clothes, and you turn a deaf ear to the cry of the poor.

51 Let all those abbey lands and glebe lands that have been given to the priests be given to the poor of the nation, and let all the great houses, abbeys, steeple houses and the Palace of Whitehall itself become houses for the care of the needy, or for some use other than they have now, so that the blind and disabled can go there and not have to go begging up and down the streets... Let all these fines that get paid to the lords of the manors be given to the poor people instead, for the lords have enough already.... Let all the poor, the blind and the disabled be provided for by the nation, so that there needn't be a beggar in England or in England's dominions.

52 O how are you daubed with silver lace, and your jewels and your spots on your faces and your feathers and your wearing of gold, and through the abundance of your vanity and of your superfluity, ambition and pride, loftiness and haughtiness stops the ear from hearing the Lord, his decree and sentence against you, and how he beholds you afar off, and stops up the eye with which you should see yourselves, and stops up your ear from hearing the poor, the blind and the lame, that lay up and down your streets; so that he that regards not the poor, regards not his Maker, and turning his ear from the poor, turns his ear from his Maker.

53 To the light of Christ Jesus in all your consciences I speak, which cannot lie, nor err, nor bear false witness, but doth bear witness for God and cries for equity, justice and righteousness to be executed.

54 But where the gospel is received indeed, strife and contention are ended, and oppression is taken off.

55 So you that the Lord hath blessed in outward things for his truth, keep over them and out of them, serving the Lord who hath blessed you, lest you be entangled. So keep above them in the righteous life and conversation, that righteousness may flow to all men in all things, honesty and truth, and that which doth justice.

56 After that riches increase take heed of setting your hearts upon them, lest they become a curse and a plague to you. For when ye were faithful at the first, the world would refrain from you and not have commerce with you; but after, when they saw ye were faithful and just in things, and righteous and honest in your tradings and dealings, then they came to have commerce and trade with you the more, because they know ye will not cozen them, nor cheat them: then ye came to have greater trading, double than ever ye had, and more than the world. But there is the danger and

52 Look how you are daubed with silver, lace and jewels, with spots on your faces, with feathers and gold to wear. Having more than enough vanity, ambition and pride, your great sense of importance dulls your sense of hearing: you cannot hear the judgment and sentence that the Lord is passing on you, or notice that he is looking at you from some way off. It dulls your sight too, so that you cannot even see yourselves. And it dulls your ear from hearing the poor, the blind and the disabled who lie along your streets. Now in disregarding the poor you disregard your maker, and in turning a deaf ear to the poor you turn a deaf ear to your maker also.

53 I'm speaking to the light of Christ Jesus which exists in the conscience of every one of you, and which is incapable of telling lies or making mistakes or bearing false witness: it bears witness for God and appeals to you to act fairly, justly and rightly.

54 But where the gospel is really accepted strife and conflict are brought to an end, and oppression is removed.

55 So you who have been blessed by the Lord in material things, for the sake of his truth, don't get involved with these things but remain detached. Do your work for the Lord, who has blessed you, so as to avoid entanglement. Be free of them by living and behaving rightly. Then the source of your right living, of your honesty and truth and justice, will flow out to everyone in everything you do.

56 When your wealth increases be careful not to set your heart on it, otherwise it will make you miserable and sick. When you first had faith the people of the world would stay away from you and not trade with you. But later, when they saw that you were reliable and just in these things, that you were honest and fair in your dealings, they came round to trading with you more: they knew that you would not defraud them or cheat them. So then your trade increased to twice what you had before, and more than other people had. But there is the danger and temptation that you might become wholly preoccupied with your business and not be able to think about anything else. You

temptation to you of drawing your minds into your business and clogging them with it; so that ye can hardly do anything to the service of God, but there will be crying, my business, my business, and your minds will go into the things and not over the things.... Then that mind that is cumbered will fret, being out of the power of God.

57 Take heed of the world's vanity and trust not in the uncertain riches, neither covet the riches of this world, but seek the kingdom of God and the righteousness thereof, and all other things will follow... so that you may be as a city set on a hill, that cannot be hid, and as lights of the world, answering the equal principle in all.

TRUST

58 Now that Friends are become a good savour in the hearts of all people, they have a friend in their house that will plead for them... And God having given them his dominion and favour, lose it not, but rather increase it in the life; for at first ye know that many could not take so much money in your trade as to buy bread with; all people stood aloof of you, when you stood upright and gave them the plain language and were at a word; but now you, through the life, having come to answer that of God in all, they say they will trust you before their own people, knowing that you will not cheat, nor wrong, nor cozen, nor oppress them. For the cry is now amongst them that are without, where is there a Quaker of such and such a trade?

59 Therefore cast your care upon him, for he cares for you: and so, as you walk in the truth, to answer the truth in your patrons and others, you will see in time, you will reach the good in them, that they will give more credit to you, and trust you more than them that disobey the spirit of God in their hearts.

will then hardly give a thought to your work for God, because you will
be thinking 'my business, my business' and your minds will get entangled in these things instead of being free of them.... The mind that is
cluttered will then get anxious, unable to draw on the power of God.

57 Be wary of worldly vanity and don't put your trust in material wealth,
which is unreliable. Don't even crave for the wealth of this world. But
set your mind on God's rule and his justice, and everything else will
then follow... then you will be like a city built on a hill that cannot
be hidden, and like lights for the world, responding to the sense of
equality that exists in everyone.

TRUST

58 Now that Friends are in good odour with everyone, they have a friend
in the house who will plead their cause.... And since God has given
you this authority and privilege, be sure you don't lose it, but try to
increase it as you live in 'the life'. For at first, as you know, there were
not many of you could make enough money from your trade to buy
bread.... You were straight with the people and you spoke to them
plainly and to the point, so they stood aloof from you. But now,
because of the life [in you], you have come to evoke that something of
God in them all, and they say they will trust you more than their own
people, knowing that you won't cheat or wrong or defraud or oppress
them. So now the talk among the people out there is this, 'Where is
there a Quaker of this or that trade?'!

59 Therefore cast all your anxiety on him, for he cares for you. And as
you live your lives in response to reality, to evoke a sense of reality in
your masters and others, you will see eventually that you do reach the
good in them, that they begin to give you more credit, and that they
trust you more than those who disobey the spirit of God in their
hearts.

GOVERNMENT

60 If thou watches thy own plantation against thieves, in thy
own way which thou art desired, for the good of thyself
and neighbours, against such as would burn thy plantation
and thy neighbour's and destroy and rob you, wilt not thou
discover this to the magistrates to punish such evil doers,
who are set for the punishing of the evil doers and execut-
ing wrath upon them and for the praise of them that do
well? Surely yes. And for this cause we pay tribute to them
and give Caesar his due, that we may live a godly and
peaceable life under them, as they are God's ministers
attending upon this very thing, to wit, the punishing of the
evil doers and the praise of them that do well; for the law
was not made for the righteous, but for the sinner and disobedient, which is good in its place.

61 All Friends everywhere that are in any sufferings, let your
sufferings be gathered up together in every county, ye that
have suffered by justices or constables or bailiffs; let your
names be set to your sufferings, and a name or two to
witness them, and the names of them that caused you to
suffer. And after that ye have gathered up your sufferings in
every county, in the county where the judges come, let
your sufferings be laid before them who are sent forth from
the head and heads of the nation (which nation or nations
is to be governed as a family, in justice and truth, and judgment and righteousness). For he that is the head of the
nation gives forth his charge to the judges, for they are all
as his servants.... The sufferings being gathered together,
short and true, and their actions that have not been just and
righteous, who caused the righteous to suffer and truth to
fall in the gates, and in the streets, that equity cannot enter
(for equity cannot enter where truth is fallen, for that
which lets in equity is truth).... And if the judge that sits in
the gate will not judge righteously, nor plead the cause of
the innocent, nor help the helpless, nor break the jaws of

GOVERNMENT

60 If you watch out for thieves on your own plantation, in the way you think best for yourself and your neighbours, and if you watch out for arsonists who are set on destroying your plantation and your neighbour's, or on robbing you, won't you pass this knowledge on to the magistrates, who are there for the purpose of punishing wrong-doers and bringing retribution on them, and of commending those who do right? Of course you will. That is why you pay taxes to them and 'give Caesar his due', so that under their protection we can live our lives peaceably and for God, since they are appointed by God for this very purpose: to punish those who do wrong and to commend those who do right. For the law was not made for those who already do right, but for those who behave badly and are disobedient, and in its place the law is a good thing.

61 All you Friends who have suffered [for your witness], wherever you are, see that accounts of your suffering are brought together in every county, you that have suffered from justices or constables or bailiffs. Include your own names in these accounts, and the names of one or two witnesses, and the names of those who made you suffer. And when you have collected these accounts from every county, i.e. the counties which the judges visit, present your accounts to those who are sent out by the head and heads of the nation – the nation after all is to be governed like a family, in justice and truth, with sound and right judgment. For the person who is head of the nation issues instructions to the judges, who all act as his servants... [so let] the reports of your suffering be brought together, short and truthful, including the actions of those who have not been just and right, but made those who are right suffer and undermined truth in the court and in the streets, so that equity was no longer possible – for equity is not possible when truth is undermined, for it's truth that makes equity possible.... And if the judge who sits in court will not judge rightly or plead the cause of the innocent or help the helpless or bring bad people to account for ripping the innocent apart, but proves to be inef-

the wicked that tear and rend the innocent (but is light and vain), God, who is just, is ready to plead their cause and to judge and cast out the unjust judges. For he that judgeth among the judges (and relieves the oppressed and helps the helpless and strengthens the weak hands and feeble knees and gives righteousness to every one that loves it, to every one whose intents are upright and single) gives true judgment agreeable to that of himself in every one, and crosses the ends and intents of every one that is from that, and gives judgment upon the unjust. And that a copy of all your sufferings, which are delivered to the judges in every county be kept and sent up to him that is the head in the nation (who sends forth the judges as his servants) that he may see, measure and weigh, how unrighteously they have judged, and what his servants have done, which cause the dividing of his family; and through the want of judgment running down the streets, equity cannot enter because truth is fallen. So these things being laid upon the heads of the nation that they may feel and see that God's judgments are just, and will come upon them if they do not judge justly, and do not measure righteously, and do not weigh truly.

62 Keep out of the restless, discontented, disquieted spirit of the world about the government, for you know it has been always our way to seek the good of all and to live peaceably under the government, and to seek their eternal good, peace and happiness in the Lord Jesus Christ and to lay our innocent sufferings before them, who have suffered as lambs and sheep and made no resistance, but have 'prayed for them that persecuted us'.

PERSECUTION

63 Great persecutions are in most counties in England and many are imprisoned in many places, and their goods spoiled.

fective and futile, then God, who is just, is prepared to plead the cause of the innocent and to judge the unjust judges, throwing them out of office if need be. Because the one who judges between the judges, the one who relieves the oppressed and helps the helpless and strengthens weak hands and feeble knees and enables everyone to do right who really wants to, whose motives are pure and sincere – he gives sound judgment, corresponding to that part of himself in every human being, and he thwarts the intents and purposes of everyone who is opposed to it, and he passes judgment on the unjust. And see that a copy of all the reports presented to the judges in each county is sent also to the head of the nation, who sends these judges out to work for him, so that he may see and register and consider how wrongly they have judged, and how their actions have brought division in his family, and how lack of judgment in our public places has made that equity impossible, because truth has been undermined. So let these things be laid on the heads of the nation so that they can see and feel that God's judgments are indeed just and will fall on them too if they do not judge justly or determine rightly or consider truly.

62 Avoid the social unrest and discontent about the government, for you know it has always been our way to seek the good of all and to live peaceably under the government, and indeed to seek their eternal good, peace and happiness in the Lord Jesus Christ, while laying before them the facts of our innocent suffering, for we have suffered like lambs and sheep without offering resistance, but have 'prayed for those who persecuted us'.

PERSECUTION

63 A great deal of persecution is taking place in most counties of England and many [Friends] have been imprisoned in many places, and their goods plundered.

64 For we here are under great persecution, betwixt thirteen and fourteen hundred in prison, an account of which hath lately been delivered to the king. Besides the great spoil and havoc which is made of Friends' goods by informers, and besides the great spoil upon the two-thirds of our estates and upon the twenty pound a month acts, and for not going to the steeple-house, and besides many are imprisoned and premunired for not swearing allegiance, both men, women, widows and maids, and many are fined and cast into prison, as rioters, for meeting to worship God. And we are kept out of our meetings in streets and highways in many places of the land, and beaten and abused. And therefore prize the liberty, both natural and spiritual, that you enjoy.

65 And the cause of all this our sufferings is not for any evil, but for things relating to the worship of our God and in obedience to his requirings of us.

66 They are not counted wise men and wise women that persecute one another about such things.... For you persecute one another about your own things that you invent, and not Christ's, for Christ's religion doth not admit of any persecution or violence, nor to hate friends or enemies, but self-religion will hate and persecute both.

67 All Friends and brethren everywhere that are imprisoned for the truth, give yourselves up in it and it will make you free, and the power of the Lord will carry you over all the persecutors.... Be faithful in the life and power of the Lord God, and be valiant for the truth on the earth and look not at your sufferings, and your imprisonments will reach to the prisoned that the persecutor prisons in himself.

68 And if any be beaten or wounded in going to meetings, or be struck or bruised in meetings, or taken out of meetings and imprisoned, let a copy of such things be taken and

64 For we are being severely persecuted here, with between thirteen and fourteen hundred in prison; an account of all this has recently been sent to the king. Besides the great plunder and destruction of Friends' goods by informers, and the plunder of two-thirds of our property and of the prescribed twenty pounds a month for not attending the steeple house, many have been imprisoned or had their goods distrained for not swearing allegiance [to the king] – both men and women, widows and unmarried girls – and many have been fined or thrown into prison as 'rioters', simply for meeting to worship God! And we are kept out of our meetings and forced onto the streets and highways in many parts of the land, and we are beaten and abused. So you who enjoy physical and spiritual liberty, be sure you appreciate it.

65 And the reason for all this suffering of ours has to do, not with some wrong we have done, but with our worship of God and our obedience to what he requires of us.

66 Men and women who persecute one another for such things are not thought of as wise ... For you persecute one another for concerns of your own, which you yourselves have invented, and not for Christ's. For Christ's religion has no room for persecution or violence, or for hatred of friend or enemy, whereas religion based on self will hate and persecute both.

67 All you Friends, brothers and sisters, who have anywhere been imprisoned for holding the truth, give yourselves up to the truth and it will set you free. And the power of the Lord will enable you to rise above your persecutors.... Be faithful in the strength of the life and power of God, and be valiant in the cause of [spreading] truth about the earth. Don't dwell on your suffering, and your imprisonment will touch that part of the persecutor that he has imprisoned in himself.

68 And if anyone is beaten or wounded on the way to meeting, or struck or injured in the meeting itself, or taken out of meeting and imprisoned, see that a report is made of all this and sent off... over the sent... under the hands of two or three witnesses, that the truth may be exalted and the power and life of God lived in. And if any Friends be summoned up by writs, or subpoenaed to appear personally to answer for tithes, let them do it, that the truth may stand over the head of the liar, which may answer the truth in every one.

69 If you do not stand now, you are as bad as such professors who stood only when the sun shined, and crept out when it was fine and fair weather, but when a storm or tempest came, then they ran creeping into their holes and corners, and skulking into by-corners and fled by back doors, who were ashamed of their religion and what they professed.

70 When they had led me to the common moss, and a multitude of people following, the constables took me and gave me a wisk over the shoulders with their willow rods, and so thrust me amongst the rude multitude which then fell upon me with their hedge stakes and clubs and staves and beat me as hard as ever they could strike on my head and arms and shoulders, and it was a great while before they beat me down and mazed me, and at last I fell down upon the wet common. There I lay a pretty space, and when I recovered myself again, and saw myself lying on a watery common and all the people standing about me, I lay a little still, and the power of the Lord sprang through me, and the eternal refreshings refreshed me, that I stood up again in the eternal power of God and stretched out my arms amongst them all, and said again with a loud voice, 'Strike again, here is my arms and my head and my cheeks.' And there was a mason, a rude fellow, a professor so-called, he gave me a blow with all his might just atop of my hand, as it was stretched out, with his walking rule-staff.... The skin was struck off my hand and a little blood came, and I looked at it in the love of God, and I was in the love of God to them all that had persecuted me.

signatures of two or three witnesses, so that the truth may be seen for what it is and people may come to live in the power and life of God. And if any Friends are served a writ or subpoenaed to appear personally for failure to pay tithes, let them go to the court and see that truth overwhelms the liar – it may then evoke the truth in every one there.

69 If you don't stand now you are no better than those Christians who stood only so long as the sun shone and crept out of hiding when the weather was fine and fair, but when a violent storm arose they ran off, creeping into their holes and hideaways, skulking into hideouts, fleeing by back doors. They were ashamed of their religion and what they claimed to believe in.

70 When they had led me onto the mossy common, with a crowd following behind, the constables took hold of me, whisked me over the shoulder with their willow rods and then thrust me into the uncivilised crowd, who fell on me with their hedge stakes, clubs and staves, and beat my head, arms and shoulders as hard as they possibly could. It was quite a while before they beat me to the ground and stunned me, but at last I fell down on the wet common. I lay there for some time, and when I recovered and saw myself lying on the wet common and the people standing around me, I lay still for a moment, and the power of the Lord sprang up within me and the eternal source refreshed me. I then stood up in the eternal power of God and stretched out my arms to them all, and I said again in a loud voice, 'Strike again. Here are my arms and my head and my cheeks'. A mason was there, a crude fellow, a believer so-called, and raising his walking stick, he gave me as big a blow as he could on top of my hand, as I was stretching it out … Skin was torn off my hand and some blood came out – I looked at it in the love of God, and I felt the love of God for all those who had persecuted me.

71 After the meeting was over and I had gone up to my room, another ambassador arrived at Pall Mall with a company of Irish colonels, a

71 There came another ambassador with a company of Irish colonels, rude men, to Pall Mall, after the meeting was done and I was gone up into a chamber. And I heard one of them say he would kill all the Quakers and Baptists and Presbyterians and Independents and Monarchy People. So I went down to him and was moved in the power of the Lord to speak to him, and it came over him. And I told him, 'The Law said, an eye for an eye and a tooth for a tooth, but thou threatens thou wilt kill all and the Quakers though they have done thee no hurt, but here is gospel for thee, here is my hair, and here is my cheek, and here are my shoulders', and turned them to him. He and his company were so amazed that they said if that was our principle, and that we were as we said, then they never saw the like in their lives. So I told him and them I was the same in life as I was in words, and the truth came so over him that he grew loving.

SUFFERING

72 Every one keep on your watch and guard against the enemy that led out from God, out of life and truth. For all the sufferings are by and through him that is out of the truth, so they that will live godly shall suffer persecution; but you that suffer in the truth, and by the contrary for the truth's sake, the spirit of glory will rest upon you.

73 All my dear friends, in the everlasting power, life and truth live, for you cannot live without it in the winds and storms. And though the hills and the mountains are burned and the trees are become fruitless and winter hath devoured the former fruits and you do see that persecution hath choked them and the heat hath scorched them, whereby the untimely figs are fallen and the corn is withered on the house-top and the night is come and the evil beasts go out of their den... truth lives, and the power of God is over them all.

74 Truth can live in the jails.

rough bunch of men. I heard one of them say he would kill all the Quakers, and the Baptists, Presbyterians, Independents and Monarchy people. So I went down to him and I was moved by the power of the Lord to say something to him, and it obviously took hold of him. I said, 'The *law* said "an eye for an eye and a tooth for a tooth", but you threaten to kill the Quakers and others though they have done you no harm. Well, here is *gospel* for you: here is my hair, here is my cheek, and here are my shoulders', and I turned them towards him. He and his company were so amazed by this that they said if that was our basis and we lived by what we said, then they never saw the like in their lives. So I told them all that I was the same in life as I was in words, and the truth so took hold of him that he grew to be loving.

SUFFERING

72 Each one of you stay awake and on your guard against the enemy that led [us] away from God, away from life and truth, for all [our] suffering comes as a result of his departing from truth. So those who want to devote their lives to God will find they have to suffer persecution. But you who do suffer in the truth, and against all reason suffer for the sake of truth, the spirit of glory will rest on you.

73 My dear friends, all of you, live in dependence on the everlasting power, life and truth, for, with the winds and storms [you have to weather], you won't be able to live without it. And though the hills and mountains have been burned [by the sun], the trees have become fruitless, winter has devoured the fruit they once had and you see that persecution has strangled them and the heat has scorched them, so that the figs have fallen before their time, the corn has withered on the house-top, night has fallen and wild animals set out from their dens... truth lives, and the power of God rises above them all.

74 Truth can live in the jails.

75 My desire is that you may all be kept alive to God and live in the living unity of the spirit, which is the bond of the heavenly peace, that passeth the knowledge of the world, which peace brings such joys which transcend all your sufferings and will carry you above them.

76 Do not think time long, nor your sufferings long, for the Lord will lay no more upon you but what you are able to bear; yea, upon his faithful people. I know it, and am a witness for God in all my sufferings and imprisonments, and haling before magistrates about sixty times, about these thirty-six years.

HOPE

77 Whilst I was in my travails and sufferings I saw the state of the city New Jerusalem which comes out of heaven.... 'Oh, this blessed city is appeared. Oh, glorious things will come to pass. You will see glorious things will come. I desire, I wish that these outward powers of the earth were given up. I can tell what to say to them. Oh, hypocrisy! It makes me sick to think of them. I have given them a visitation and as faithful a warning as ever was. There is an ugly a slubbering hound, an ugly hound, an ugly slubbering hound. But the Lord forgive them – destruction, destruction'.

78 The mighty day of the Lord is come and coming that all hearts shall be made manifest, the secrets of everyone's heart shall be revealed with the light of Jesus, which cometh from Jesus Christ, who lighteneth every man that cometh into the world.

79 Ye do well that ye take heed unto the light that shines in the dark place until the day dawn and the day star arise in your hearts.

80 By the power of the Lord ye have overcome, and in the

75 My desire is that you will all be kept alive to God and live [together] in the living unity of the spirit, for that is the bond of heavenly peace that surpasses what the world can know, and that peace will give you a joy that transcends all your suffering and will lift you above it.

76 Don't think how long it takes, how long your suffering must go on, because the Lord won't lay on you more than you can bear – you, his faithful people. I know this, and I can bear witness for God in all my suffering, having been imprisoned and dragged into court some sixty times in all these thirty-six years.

HOPE

77 Some time during my ordeal and my suffering I had a vision of the city of New Jerusalem, coming down from heaven.... 'Oh, this happy city has appeared. Wonderful things will happen. You will see wonderful things happening. I desire, I wish that these external authorities of the earth were abandoned. I know what to say to them. Oh, hypocrisy! It makes me sick to think of them. I have given them an opportunity and as truthful a warning as they ever had. I see an ugly, slobbering dog, an ugly dog, an ugly slobbering dog. May the Lord forgive them – destruction, destruction.'

78 A day is coming, and has come, the mighty day of the Lord, when everyone's heart will be disclosed, the secrets of everyone's heart will be revealed by the light of Jesus – the light which comes from Jesus Christ who enlightens everyone who comes into the world.

79 You do well to pay attention to the light that shines in the dark place, until day breaks and the morning star rises in your hearts.

80 You have overcome already by the power of the Lord, and by the power of the Lord you will overcome, overcome everything, and with that power you will stand secure, when everything opposed to you has [finally] gone.

power of the Lord ye will overcome all, and in it will stand, when all the contrary is gone.

81 With that power of God ye will answer the witness of God in all and bring them to that, that with that they may have a part in the kingdom of God, and a share with you of the same, in which ye will have peace, life, joy, dominion and prosperity. And so it will be your life to do good and to beget into life, up to God; and in that power that doth so ye will not labour in vain.

82 All my dear friends, folly and wickedness will have an end, but the word of the Lord will have no end, it endures for ever.

83 And we are to hold fast this hope that is set before us, which we have as an anchor of the soul, both sure and steadfast.

THE VISION

84   Dear friends,
         With my love to you in the holy peaceable truth
                 that never changes,
                 nor admits of evil,
         but makes all free
                 that receive it
                 and that walk in it,
         and is over all the clouds without rain
                 and wells without water
                 and trees without fruit.
         And from the truth floweth justice,
                 equity, righteousness and godliness,
                 mercy and tenderness,
         that brings a man's heart, mind, soul and spirit
                 to the infinite and
                 incomprehensible God,
         and from it a love flows
                 to all the universal creation

81 With that power of God you will evoke the witness of God in everyone and bring them to accept it, so that, accepting it, they can share
with you in the kingdom of God. And there you will all find peace, life,
joy, power and prosperity. So your life will be about doing good and
begetting life [in others], bringing them close to God. And the power
that enables you to do this will ensure that you do not labour in vain.

82 My dear friends, all of you, folly and wickedness will come to an end,
but the word of the Lord has no end: it endures for ever.

83 And we should grasp this hope set before us, for that hope is an
anchor for our lives, safe and secure.

THE VISION

84 Dear friends,
   My love to you in the holy peaceable truth
      that never changes,
      or tolerates evil,
   but sets everyone free
      who receives it
      and lives by it.
   It is above all clouds without rain
      and wells without water
      and trees without fruit.
   And from the truth flows justice,
      equity, rightness, devotion,
      mercy and tenderness.
   It brings the human heart, mind, soul and spirit
      to the infinite and
      incomprehensible God.
   And from it a love flows
      to the whole creation,

and would have all to come
    to the knowledge of the truth,
and it bends every one to their utmost ability
    to serve God and his truth
    and to spread it abroad,
and it brings their minds out of the earth,
    which makes them brittle
    and changeable and uncertain,
for it doth not change,
    neither doth it touch with
    that which does change.
As to unity, it makes all
    like itself
    that do obey it,
universal, to live out of
    narrowness and self,
    and deny it.
So it brings all into oneness
    and answereth the good principle
    of God in all people,
and brings into humility
    and the fear of the Lord,
    which is the beginning of wisdom,
and it brings all to have a care
    of God's glory
    and his honour,
and watches over all the professors of it
    for their good,
    to keep within its bounds
    and walk within its order,
which he that is out of truth
    leads into all disorder,
    in whom there is no truth,
and the truth makes all its children
    free from him
    and in it to reign over him.
Thanks, glory and honour

a love that wants everyone
    to come to know the truth.
It bends everyone with all their might
    to work for God and his truth
    and to make it widely known.
It weans them from material things,
    which make them liable to change,
    unstable and unsure,
but truth does not change,
    it's not even affected by
    what does change.
As for unity, it makes everyone
    like itself,
    who obeys it,
and universal, to live their lives free
    of the narrowness of self,
    and reject it.
So it leads everyone to oneness,
    evokes the good divine source
    of life in everyone,
and leads people to humility
    and reverence for the Lord,
    the beginning of wisdom,
and leads everyone to have a care
    for God's glory
    and his honour,
and keeps an eye on everyone
    who believes in it,
    to stay within its bounds
    and live within its order,
whilst the one who has abandoned truth
    brings only disorder,
    because they lack truth,
but truth sets all its children
    free from him,
    in truth to rule over him.
Thanks, glory and honour

to the Lord God of truth
over all for ever.
Amen.

The Lord, who is the God of all peace and order, alone pro-tects and preserves his people with his eternal power, for the devil's power is not eternal; it had a beginning and must have an ending, for the eternal power limits that devourer and destroyer. And therefore, friends, patience must be exercised in the truth; and keep to the word of patience, which word was before the world was, and abides and endures for ever, and it will keep Friends over and out of all the snares of the world and its temptations.

So with my love in the seed of life, that reigns over all, and in it the Lord God Almighty preserve and keep you all to his glory. Amen.

G.F.

to the Lord God of truth
over all for ever.
Amen.

The Lord, the God of all peace and order, he alone protects and preserves his people with his eternal power, for the power of the devil is not eternal; it had a beginning and must have an ending, for the eternal power sets a limit to that devourer and destroyer. And therefore, friends, you need to be patient in the truth: stick to the word that is patience itself, the word that existed before the world began, that is still here now and will be with us for ever, and that word will keep Friends above and beyond the snares of the world and its many temptations.

So, my love to you all in the seed of life that rules over all. May the Lord God Almighty preserve you in the seed and keep you all to his glory. Amen.

G.F.

ENDNOTES for part three

1. *Journal* (for 1648), ed. Nickalls, pp.27f. Cf. Genesis 3:24.
2. Manuscript 61E Aa (1669), bound with the Annual Catalogue of George Fox's papers, available in Friends House Library, London; quoted by Hugh McGregor Ross, ed., *George Fox speaks for himself*, Sessions, York, 1991, p.17. 'Under curtains' probably means 'under the sky' as in Psalm 104:2 and Isaiah 40:22, where God 'stretcheth out the heavens as a curtain'. For 'garnished the heavens' cf. Job 26:13.
3. Epistle 216 (1661), *Works* 7:216f.
4. Epistle 240 (1664), *Works* 7:269f. For the allusions to the creation story cf. Genesis 1:28; 3:16f. See Glossary on 'the fall' and 'the curse'.
5. Epistle 82 (1655), *Works* 7:93.
6. Epistle 33 (1653), *Works* 7:40. Cf. Proverbs 3:19; John 1:1-3. The quotation is from Psalm 24:1.
7. Epistle 32 (1653), *Works* 7:38. On the connection between 'image of God' and 'kings' see Genesis 1:26-28. A king at that time – the writing of the biblical story – was widely believed to have been created in the image of God, as God's representative on earth. See Glossary on 'image'.
8. Epistle 215 (1661), *Works* 7:215.
9. 'To all that would know the way to the kingdom' (1653), in *Doctrinals*, *Works* 4:16.
10. Epistle of 1654, in *Journal*, ed. Nickalls, p.175.
11. Epistle 54 (1653), *Works* 7:69.

12. Epistle 135 (1657), *Works* 7:132.
13. Epistle 218 (1662), *Works* 7:221.
14. Epistle 43 (1653), *Works* 7:52.
15. Epistle 351 (1678), *Works* 8:149.
16. Epistle 366 (1682), *Works* 8:193f. Cf. John 1:9; 12:36; Ephesians 5:8.
17. Epistle 73 (1654), *Works* 7:83.
18. Epistle 217 (1662), *Works* 7:220.
19. Epistle 76 (1654), *Works* 7:86.
20. Epistle 166 (1658), *Works* 7:155.
21. Epistle 384 (1683), *Works* 8:231.
22. Epistle 195 (1660), *Works* 7:185.
23. Epistle 406 (1685), *Works* 8:293.
24. Epistle 405 (1685), *Works* 8:292.
25. Epistle 169 (1658), *Works* 7:157f. Cf. Amos 5:10 for 'reproving in the gate', which in the Bible referred to courts held 'in the gate' of the city wall.
26. Epistle 55 (1653), *Works* 7:70.
27. Epistle 18 (1652), *Works* 7:25f.
28. Epistle 111 (1655), *Works* 7:110.
29. Epistle 191 (1660), *Works* 7:182.
30. Epistle 215 (1661), *Works* 7:216.
31. Epistle 48 (1653), *Works* 7:63.
32. Epistle 53 (1653), *Works* 7:68. Cf. 1 Peter 3:1,2.
33. Epistle 232 (1664), *Works* 7:249.
34. Epistle 215 (1661), *Works* 7:216. Cf. Philippians 4:5.
35. Epistle 53 (1653), *Works* 7:68.
36. Epistle 200 (1661), *Works* 7:192-6. For the quotation on 'doing truth', which seems to be a combination of two biblical texts, cf. John 3:21; 1 John 1:6; 1 Peter 1:17.
37. A letter 'to Friends in the ministry', 1656, in *Journal*, ed. Nickalls, p.263.
38. Epistle 315 (1675), *Works* 8:75.

39. Epistle 318 (1675), *Works* 8:85.
40. A paper of 1654, in *Doctrinals, Works* 4:46.
41. Epistle 263 (1668), *Works* 7:328.
42. A declaration to the king, 1660, in *Journal*, ed. Nickalls, pp.399f. This text was written by Fox and a number of other leading Friends.
43. *Journal* (for 1650), ed. Ellwood, in *Works* 1:113. Cf. James 4:1-3.
44. *Journal* (for 1660), ed. Ellwood, in *Works* 1:408. The quotation is from John 18:36.
45. A paper of 1661, in *Journal*, ed. Nickalls, p.417.
46. Epistle 242 (1665), *Works* 7:272. Cf. Ephesians 6:10-17.
47. Epistle 249 (1667), *Works* 7:284f. The rough quotation is from Philippians 4:11.
48. Epistle 200 ('on justice', 1661), *Works* 7:192-195.
49. 'The vials of the wrath of God poured forth upon the Man of Sin' (1654?), in *Doctrinals, Works* 4:29. For 'the earth is the Lord's...' see Psalm 24:1.
50. A paper of 1657, in *Journal*, ed. Nickalls, p.311.
51. *To the Parliament of the Commonwealth of England, Fifty-nine Particulars laid down for the Regulating Things,* 1659, in the Bevan-Naish Library, Woodbrooke, Birmingham, bound with other tracts under A.5.19 (53); not since published.
52. 'To the high and lofty ones' (1655), in *Doctrinals, Works* 4:49f.
53. A paper 'to the heads and governors of this nation', 1658, in *Journal*, ed. Ellwood, in *Works* 1:378.
54. A paper of 1665, in *Journal*, ed. Nickalls, p.488. See Glossary on 'gospel'.
55. Epistle 232 (1664), *Works* 7:249.
56. Epistle 131 (1656), *Works* 7:126.
57. Epistle 250 (1667), *Works* 7:300f. Cf. Matthew 5:14-16; 6:33; Philippians 2:15.
58. Epistle 251 (1667), *Works* 7:301f.
59. Epistle 391 (1684), *Works* 8:249. Cf. 1 Peter 5:7.

60. Epistle 319 ('to Friends in Nevis and the Carribee Islands', 1675), *Works* 8:87f. On 'punishing' and 'praising' cf. 1 Peter 2:13f; on giving 'Caesar his due' cf. Luke 20:21-25.

61. Epistle 141 (1657), *Works* 7:135f.

62. Epistle 369 (1681), *Works* 8:199. The rough quotation is from Matthew 5:44.

63. Epistle 315 ('to Friends in Barbados', 1675), *Works* 8:75.

64. Epistle 386 ('to Friends in Charleston in Carolina', 1683), *Works* 8:233f.

65. *Journal* (for 1661), ed. Nickalls, p.421.

66. Epistle 249 (1667), *Works* 7:297.

67. Epistle 92 (1655), *Works* 7:100. On 'truth... make you free' cf. John 8:32.

68. Epistle 140 (1657), *Works* 7:134.

69. Epistle 289 (1672), *Works* 8:38.

70. *Journal* (for 1652), ed. Nickalls, pp.127f.

71. *Journal* (for 1661), ed. Nickalls, pp.409f.

72. Epistle 223 (1662), *Works* 7:238. Cf. 2 Timothy 3:12; 1 Peter 4:14.

73. Epistle 236 (1664), *Works* 7:258.

74. Epistle 227 (1663), *Works* 7:241.

75. Epistle 345 (1677), *Works* 8:143. Cf. Philippians 4:7.

76. Epistle 377 (1682), *Works* 8:215. Cf. 1 Corinthians 10:13.

77. *Journal*, ed. Nickalls, p.575, in which Fox quotes a paper of the time, 1671, describing his vision. Cf. the vision of John in Revelation 21:1-5.

78. A paper of 1656 written with Edward Pyott and William Salt, in *Journal*, ed. Nickalls, p.236.

79. A paper of 1657, in *Journal*, ed. Nickalls, p.318. See Glossary on 'day star'.

80. Epistle 207 (1661), *Works* 7:207.

81. Epistle 217 (1662), *Works* 7:219.

82. Epistle 160 (1658), *Works* 7:152. Cf. 1 Peter 1:22-25.

83. 'Concerning the antiquity of the people of God called
   Quakers' (1689), in *Doctrinals*, *Works* 6:390. Cf. Hebrews 6:18f.
84. The whole of Epistle 358 (1679), *Works* 8:165. I have versified
   the text to bring out the poetic structure of his writing here,
   or more likely, of his spoken delivery. On the 'incantatory style'
   of George Fox, which enhanced his 'fluency in spontaneous
   oral composition', see Richard Bauman, *Let your words be few:
   symbolism of speaking and silence among seventeenth-century Quakers*, Cambridge University Press, 1983, pp.75-78.

GLOSSARY

GLOSSARY

A number of words used by Fox have changed their meaning since his time, or simply lost a meaning they once had. I am therefore appending a list of the most important of these words with an indication of the meaning they would have had to Fox. I have included also some words to which Fox gave a distinctive meaning of his own. In establishing these meanings I have drawn on the full-length *Oxford English Dictionary* (OUP), which helpfully gives examples of seventeenth-century use; Aimo Seppänen, *The Inner Light in the journals of George Fox: a semantic study* (University of Tampere, Finland, 1975), a study of some 83 words and phrases; Joseph Pickvance, *A reader's companion to George Fox's journal* (QHS, London, 1989); Howard Alexander, *A glossary of words and phrases most commonly used by George Fox* (Friends United Press, Richmond, Indiana, 1983), which relies on internal evidence for establishing meanings; T. Canby Jones (ed.), *The power of the Lord is over all: the pastoral letters of George Fox* (Friends United Press, Richmond, Indiana, 1989); C.T. Onions and R.D. Eagleson, *A Shakespeare glossary* (OUP, 1986); and Basil Willey, *The seventeenth century background: studies in the thought of the age in relation to poetry and religion* (Penguin, 1962, first published in 1934). The most important source for understanding Fox's use of a word is the English Bible of 1611 (the so-called Authorised Version); I have therefore freely quoted from the Bible when that seemed to give a clue to Fox's sense, and always from the 1611 translation, unless indicated otherwise.

abroad In general it meant widely, broadly (as in 2:81), but it could also mean away from home, out of doors (and not simply away from the home country, as in modern use). Thus 1:1. Cf. 'gad' and 'forth' below.

anointing Fox's use is clearly influenced by 1 John 2:26f: 'These things have I written unto you concerning them that seduce you. But the anointing which ye have received of him abideth in you, and ye need not that any man teach you: but as the same anointing teacheth you of all things, and is truth, and is no lie, and even as it hath taught you, ye shall abide in him.' An anointing is literally a pouring of oil on the body, but it was used in the ancient world as a symbolic act of empowerment for a priest or king. A king could therefore be known as 'the anointed' (cf. meaning of 'Christ'). By extension it could also be used for the spiritual act of being empowered by God. Cf. J. Daus in 1561, 'Oil is a resemblance of the holy Ghost, wherefore St. John calleth also the holy Ghost an anointing'[1.]

answer There are two meanings in Fox's time which are relevant to his special use of this word. To answer is (1) to respond in word or action to someone or something else: e.g. in Milton an 'echo' can be an answer: 'With other echo late I taught your shades to answer'[2]; and (2) to imitate, match, correspond to what is done by someone or something else: e.g. in 1793 Holcroft 'to answer wit with reason is like endeavouring to hold an eel by the tail'[3]. So when Fox urges Friends 'to answer that of God' in people he is saying two things: *respond* to that of God in them, because that is how God will work in them, and do so by *corresponding* to that of God, that is, by speaking and acting in harmony with this light and life in them. This is most clearly exemplified in 3:20, 'And so, living in the light and truth ye may answer the light and truth in every man and woman'. However, responding implies something has already been done by the other; this makes sense when we realise that 'that of God'

in Fox is an abbreviation for 'that of God which acts in people'
in some way, what he elsewhere calls 'the witness of God' in
people or 'the word of God' (cf. 'that of God' below). We are
called to respond to what God is already saying or doing in
people, even when they are not aware of it themselves. Indeed,
the point of answering is precisely to make people aware of it.
And his use often seems to imply that 'answering' that of God
in people will in turn evoke an 'answer' from them (see e.g.
3:16,17,19), that is, help people to recognise that of God in
themselves and to act in response to it. A close parallel in
modern use would be 'answering someone's need'.

antichrist A human enemy or opponent of Christ (as distinct from
the devil, below, who was the spiritual enemy), as in 1 John
2:18,22; 2 John 7. To Fox antichrists would have been people
who opposed the light within.

apostasy 'The apostasy' was specifically the 'falling away' of the
Christian church from the original spirit and life of the apostles.

at a word To be 'at a word' is to be brief; literally, to rely on the
utterance of a single word. Cf. William Penn in 1694 'They were
at a word in dealing; nor could their customers' many words
tempt them from it'[4].

brittle In a figurative sense it meant either (1) liable to break
faith, inconstant, fickle, or (2) weak, insecure, unstable, as e.g.
in W. Fenner in 1657, 'Consider how brittle your hearts are'[5].

canker To infect with a running sore, or (figuratively) to corrupt
the spirit.

carnal Not 'sexual' in Fox, but more generally 'fleshly, sensual',
therefore the opposite of spiritual. Cf. E. Gibbon (1781): 'Judge
whether Martin was supported by the aid of miraculous
powers, or of carnal weapons'[6]. It sometimes suggests an active
opposition to the spiritual, following the Bible, Romans 8:7,
'The carnal mind is enmity against God', as in Milton (1667),
'Had not doubt and carnal fear that day dimmed Adam's eye'[7].

Christ   Originally a title given to Jesus of Nazareth, meaning literally 'the anointed' (see above), that is 'the one empowered by God', it became a name both for the man Jesus and for the eternal son of God who became human in Jesus. In Fox it nearly always carries this strong theological meaning: Christ is 'the word of God' or 'the light of God' by which God created the world and communicates with human beings, bringing them to an awareness and experience of God. So in Fox, Christ can be said to be both the source of creation itself and also the divine light in every human being (cf. 1:99).

clear   Applied to things, or 'conditions', it would mean transparent, 'allowing light to pass through' (OED), allowing a 'clear view'. Applied to humans it could have three meanings (in Fox's writing): (1) to be unclouded in one's vision or free from confusion, (2) to be free from fault or guilt, therefore innocent (cf. Authorised Version of the Bible, 2 Corinthians 7:11, 'In all things ye have approved yourselves to be clear in this matter'), and (3) free from an encumbrance or an entanglement, free of a burden (cf. Shakespeare's *Merchant of Venice*, I.i.134, 'How to get clear of all the debts I owe', and W Blackstone, 'Thus the bankrupt becomes a clear man again'[8]). This last meaning survives in modern use in phrases such as 'stand clear', 'steer clear'.

comprehend   To hold, contain, or specifically 'to hold with the mind', that is, to understand, to 'take in'. Cf. John Donne in 1628: 'To comprehend is to know a thing as well as that thing can be known'[9]. Fox is particularly influenced, again, by John's Gospel: 'The light shineth in darkness; and the darkness comprehended it not' (1:5).

condition   (1) Mode of being or state, as in our modern 'medical condition' or 'in bad condition' when someone is not well, (2) state in regard to wealth, circumstances, rank or social position; e.g. Shakespeare, *The tempest*, III.i.59, 'I am in my condition a prince', and The Book of Common Prayer, 56, 'All sorts and conditions of men'. Either meaning can refer to a person's 'spiritual condition'. The plural 'conditions' was common in the seventeenth century, and could refer to either state or circumstances.

conscience   Consciousness of right and wrong, moral sense, as in Milton, in 1667, where God says of Adam and Eve, 'I will place within them as a guide my umpire conscience'[10]; and J. Butler, in 1725, 'This faculty of conscience... was placed within to be our proper governor; to direct and regulate all under principles, passions and motives of action. This is its right and office: thus sacred its authority'[11].

conversation   Before it meant 'talk with' it meant 'live with', i.e. behaviour, manner of life; 'manner of conducting oneself in the world or in society' (OED). Cf. Psalm 50:23, 'To him that ordereth his conversation aright will I shew the salvation of God'; 1 Peter 1:15, 'As he which hath called you is holy, so be ye holy in all manner of conversation'.

covenant   In general, 'a mutual agreement between two or more persons to do or refrain from doing certain acts; a contract' (OED). In the English Bible of 1611, from which Fox draws his own understanding, it is an engagement entered into by God with one or more people, e.g. with Abraham in Genesis 17:7, 'I will establish my covenant between me and thee and thy seed after thee in their generations for an everlasting covenant, to be a God unto thee, and to thy seed after thee'. In contrast to this covenant the prophets made promise of a new covenant to be written in people's hearts, Jeremiah 31:31, which the first Christian writers believed to have been fulfilled in the coming of Jesus (Galatians 4:24; Hebrews 8:13; 9:15). The Puritan writers of the seventeenth century made much of this, contrasting the 'covenant of life' with Adam and the 'covenant of grace' with Christ, which is the immediate background to Fox's use. Cf. the Puritans' *Shorter catechism*, 'When God created man he entered into a covenant of life with him, upon condition of perfect obedience'[12]; and their *Westminster larger catechism* both of 1647, 'The covenant of grace was made with Christ the second Adam, and with him all the elect as his seed'[13]. Fox, though, dropped the Puritan idea of election, implied in the covenant of grace, and preferred to speak of the 'covenant of light', drawing on Isaiah 42:6; 49:6. 'In this way', says Seppänen, '"covenant" becomes coterminous with Christ or the Inward Light'.

cozen To cheat, defraud; to deceive.

creature Anything created, not just animals. Cf. R. Brooke in 1641, 'Light was one of the first creatures'[14]. Even humans can be creatures: 'I shall despair, there is no creature loves me' (Shakespeare, *Richard III*, V.iii.200).

cumber To block up, hinder freedom of action, as in Tindale's translation of the Bible in 1534, 'Cut it down; why cumbreth it the ground?' (Luke 13:7), which may lie behind Fox's phrase in 3:26.

curse It is either the word consigning someone to a state of suffering and misery, or the state itself. It is therefore the opposite of 'blessing'. Fox often implies a reference to the curse on Adam and Eve in the story of the fall (see below) which is reversed by the blessing of Christ (e.g. in 3:4), returning people to the original blessing of creation. Cf. Genesis 1:28; 3:14-19.

darkness 'Figuratively, a want of spiritual or intellectual light' (OED). Cf. W. Tyndale in 1531, 'All that lie in ignorance are called darkness'[15], and E. Walker in 1692, 'Truth's still in darkness undiscovered'[16].

day star The morning star, as in 2 Peter 1:19, 'We have also a more sure word of prophecy, whereunto ye do well to take heed, as unto a light that shineth in a dark place, until the day dawn, and the day star arise in your hearts'.

devil It derives from the Greek *diabolos*, which means 'the slanderer', 'the one who misrepresents or leads astray'. In Fox 'the devil' is still the semi-mythical figure of the Bible (and of his contemporary Milton), the supreme spirit of evil and the enemy of humankind, opposed dramatically to the figure of Christ (see above).

discover To uncover, expose to view, reveal, make known.

earth, earthy The earth, as the abode of human beings, was contrasted with heaven, the abode of God. 'Earthy' could therefore be characteristic of earthly as opposed to heavenly existence (cf. 1:127), as in G. Chapman in 1615, 'The impious race of earthy giants, that would heaven outface'[17]. Fox's fondness for the word probably derives from Paul in 1 Corinthians 15:47, referring to Adam, 'The first man is of the earth, earthy; the second man is the Lord from heaven'. 'Earthy' can, of course, also mean grossly material or coarse.

end (1) the close of a period of time, as in Fox's 'end of outward preaching' (2:37), (2) an intended result, aim, or purpose, e.g. J. Preston in 1628, 'A right end never had a crooked rule leading to it'[18].

evil The antithesis of good; whatever is totally unacceptable or undesirable; whatever causes unnecessary suffering.

experimental We would now say 'experiential', since 'experimental' in the seventeenth century referred to the whole range of experience, and not just to the disciplined testing of the scientific method. Fox's meaning is captured by R. Harvey in 1593, 'Trusting none, but which they find certainly, and experimentally true'[19], and by Bishop Hall in 1644, speaking of 'those solid divines that experimentally know what belongs to the healing of a sinful soul'[20]. However, Fox used the word to indicate how he came to a knowledge of the truth and he suggested elsewhere (see section on 'experience', 1:13-22) that others might test this truth by undergoing a similar experience, so in effect he included our modern sense of 'experiment' in his use of the word.

fall The 'fall' of human beings from the high state in which they were created, and thus their alienated state afterwards, symbolised in their banishment from paradise (in the story in Genesis 3). So humans can be said to be 'in the Fall' or, if they recover their connection with God, to be 'before the Fall was' (cf. 3:1).

fear 'A mingled feeling of dread and reverence towards God' (OED), e.g. in the 1611 Bible, Psalm 111:10, 'The fear of the Lord is the beginning of wisdom'.

form (1) a prescribed way of doing things, as in Shakespeare's *Much ado*, 'The plain form of marriage' (IV.i.2), or (2) a set order of words, such as a prayer book; cf. *The pilgrimage of perfection* in 1526, 'Our lord and saviour Jesu Christ hath given us a form how to pray'[21]. That this is how Fox understands the word is clear from 2:38, but he also broadens its meaning to refer to all structures of religion, and in this broad sense the 'form' of religion is often contrasted with the 'power' (see below), following 2 Timothy 3:1-5: 'In the last days perilous times shall come, for men shall be lovers of their own selves... more than lovers of God, having a form of godliness, but denying the power thereof; from such turn away'. Uncharacteristically, he allows himself at one point – a very early text – to speak of 'the spirit's form' (2:39).

forth 'Out' in modern English. It is often a simplification of 'go forth', i.e. 'go out', as in Shakespeare's *Coriolanus* (I.iii.99), 'Indeed, I will not forth'. Cf. 'out' and 'abroad'.

Friends The first followers and companions of Fox were known as 'Friends in the truth', deriving the sense from John 15:14f, where Jesus says to his disciples, 'Ye are my friends, if ye do whatsoever I command you. Henceforth I call you not servants; for the servant knoweth not what his lord doeth; but I have called you friends; for all things that I have heard of my Father I have made known unto you'.

from Often a short form of a much stronger phrase such as 'away from' or 'quite apart from'. If someone is 'from the truth' they have clearly abandoned it. Cf. the similar use of 'out of' (below).

gad To wander from place to place, restlessly, usually without serious intent. Cf. T. Boston in 1732, 'gadding abroad to satisfy her youthful curiosity'[22]. It could have the figurative sense of wandering from the true path, e.g. in Milton, 'While we leave the Bible to gad after these traditions'[23]. Fox could even have had both senses in mind: he wanted to warn people not to wander from the truth within them, which meant not wandering from one preacher to another, one sect to another, looking for the truth elsewhere. Cf. 'abroad' and extracts 1:1; 1:123.

generation Sometimes, offspring, descendants, posterity; not always the modern sense of people born at the same time (as in 1:103).

go into It can mean 'to take part in, to join in'. Cf. G. Burnet in 1688, 'Those who are discontented do naturally go into every new thing that... promises relief'[24]. Cf. 'into' and 'run into' below.

gospel Fox seems to have given his own meaning to this word, perhaps from a misreading of Romans 1:16: 'I am not ashamed of the gospel of Christ; for it is the power of God unto salvation'. He understands 'the gospel' to be equivalent to 'the power of God', and when he uses the word 'gospel' he usually adds 'the power of God' to make his meaning clear. He rarely seems to use it in its original sense of 'the message', referring specifically to the Christian message about the coming of Jesus Christ (but cf. 1:2), perhaps because he wanted to de-emphasise the formal proclamation of words ('outward preaching') in favour of 'the word' which is spoken in people's hearts, and which is indeed 'the power of God'. Cf. the Quaker theologian Robert Barclay in 1676: 'This saving spiritual light is the gospel, which the apostle saith expressly is preached in every creature under heaven... For the gospel is not a mere declaration of good things, being the power of God unto salvation to all those that believe, Rom. 1.16. Though the outward declaration of the gospel be taken sometimes for the gospel, yet it is but figuratively, and by a metonymy. For to speak properly, the gospel is this inward power and life which preacheth glad tidings in the hearts of all men, offering salvation unto them'[25].

gospel order The ordered life of a community arising from the acceptance by each individual of the light or word within them, the gospel (see above), rather than from an authoritative person or book.

grace An enabling power by which people can respond to the truth and live by it. The Puritans of Fox's day made a sharp distinction between the grace that is given to everyone, but which is unable to 'save them from sin', and the special grace given to some that does save them. Fox ignored this distinction, emphasising that grace was both universal and saving. Cf. Titus 2:11-12 for his source.

habitation(s) A place of abode or residence, whether a country or a house. Cf. J. Davies in 1662, 'They had no cities nor settled habitations, but lived in woods'[26]. Coverdale had the figurative sense used often by Fox in his translation of Habakkuk 3:11, 'The sun and moon remained still in their habitations'.

image It can mean 'a likeness' in general, as in our modern use, or the specific 'likeness to God' which exists in human beings, in which case it is yet another reference to 'that of God' in human beings. But there is also the implication, drawn from the New Testament, that human beings can 'grow up in the image' of God, that the original image, obscured by 'the fall' (see above), can be restored to its first glory. Cf. Genesis 1:26, 'And God said, Let us make man in our image, after our likeness', and Colossians 3:9f, 'Ye have... put on the new man, which is renewed in knowledge after the image of him that created him'. See also 'measure' below.

imagination It has the negative connotation that was usual in the seventeenth century, indicating the human faculty for producing images or ideas that misrepresent reality, 'often with the implication that the conception does not correspond to the reality of things; hence freq. *vain, false imagination*' (OED). Cf. Genesis 8:21, 'The Lord said in his heart, I will not again curse the ground any more for man's sake; for the imagination of man's heart is evil from his youth', and Luke 1:51, 'He hath scattered the proud in the imagination of their hearts'.

immediate   In actual contact or direct personal relation, with no intervening agent or medium; in relation to human awareness, '(*philos.*) a knowledge of self-evident truth; intuitive knowledge, as distinguished from that arrived at by means of demonstration or proof' (OED).

into   Fox seems to have had a peculiar sense of his own, not far removed from a very modern sense: to be 'into' something is to be involved in it and committed to it (see 3:56, where it is contrasted with being 'over' something). We might say, similarly, 'I'm really into that'. Cf. 'Go into' above, and 'run into'.

invention   Human invention is contrasted with what has been established by God. Cf. Psalm 106:29, where the worship of human-made idols is decried as an invention: 'They [our fathers] joined themselves also unto Baalpeor, and ate the sacrifices of the dead. Thus they provoked him [God] to anger with their inventions: and the plague brake in upon them'.

inward   Situated within, internal, inner; figuratively, of the heart, mind or spirit, e.g. Psalm 51:6, 'Behold, Thou desirest truth in the inward parts'. Cf. 'outward' below.

jangle   Argue, quarrel, excitedly or noisily; e.g. Milton, 'It is not worth while to jangle about a French word'[27].

let   (1) To allow, as in modern use, or (2) to hinder, prevent, stand in the way – the opposite of the modern meaning! Cf. T. Cogan in 1584, 'Much meat eaten at night grieveth the stomach, and letteth natural rest'[28]. Curiously, an example of both meanings can be found in 1:13. The second is probably an allusion to Isaiah 43:13, where God says, 'I will work, and who shall let it?'

life The spiritual condition of being alive, in contrast to the condition of spiritual death. The word can also mean 'the divinely implanted power or principle by which this condition is produced' (OED), which is in fact the central idea in Fox. So 'the life' becomes yet another reference to 'that of God' within people, but describing a different aspect. It applies especially to the experience of meeting. Cf. 'the seed' below.

light 'The light within' would normally have been understood as a natural capacity for understanding and insight, like reason or conscience, but Fox differed from most in saying it was a special, divine capacity, a function of the Spirit of God within people, which enabled them, for example, to 'see themselves'. He was anticipated by writers such as Francis Rous, who wrote in the 1630s and 1640s, e.g. 'The soul has two eyes – one human reason, the other far excelling that, a divine and spiritual Light... By it the soul doth see spiritual things as truly as the corporal eye doth corporal things' [29]. Fox followed closely the Gospel of John on this theme, especially the Prologue (1:1-18, e.g. v.9: 'That was the true light, which lighteth every man that cometh into the world'; but cf. John 3:19f, 12:35f).

low Humble in disposition, lowly, meek; as in Shakespeare's *Cymbeline*, IV.ii.249: 'That angel of the world doth make distinction of place 'tween high and low' (1611); to 'lie low' is not to keep quiet, as in the modern sense, but to live humbly, .

mass house A building for the saying of masses, i.e. a church, as would normally have been understood. But Fox would not use the word 'church' for a mere building. Cf. 2:10 and 'steeple house' below.

mazed Dazed, stupefied, (fig.) bewildered.

measure It can mean a quantity of something bestowed on a person, or an extent not to be exceeded; a limit. For use of the first cf. W. Allen in 1674, 'Men's differences about these points proceed… from their different measures of light and understanding' [30], and for the second, J. Pearson in 1659, 'What bounds can we set unto that grief, what measures to that anguish?' [31]. Fox probably drew his understanding from the Bible, e.g. Romans 12:3, 'I say… to every man that is among you, not to think of himself more highly than he ought to think; but to think soberly, according as God hath dealt to every man the measure of faith'; and Ephesians 4:7, 'Unto everyone of us is given grace according to the measure of the gift of Christ'; and 4:11-13,16, 'He gave some, apostles; and some, prophets… for the perfecting of the saints, for the work of the ministry, for the edifying of the body of Christ; till we all come in the unity of the faith, and of the knowledge of the Son of God, unto a perfect man, unto the measure of the stature of the fulness of Christ… from whom the whole body fitly joined together and compacted by that which every joint supplieth, according to the effective working in the measure of every part, making increase of the body unto the edifying of itself in love'. Seppänen comments: 'In Fox… "measure" is that quantity or amount of the Divine which is given to people, it varies with individuals but by turning to live in union with it every man can increase his measure. In Christ the Divine dwelled in its fullest measure, therefore "the measure of Christ"… means the state of perfection' (p.136f).

meat Anything eaten as food, a meal.

meet-helps Suitable companions. Cf. Genesis 2:18-22: 'And the Lord God said, It is not good that man should be alone; I will make him an help meet for him. And out of the ground the Lord God formed every beast of the field… but for Adam there was not found an help meet for him. And the Lord God… made he a woman, and brought her unto the man'.

mind In the imperative mood: 'be aware, notice; pay attention to;

give heed to; bear in mind'. Cf. Shakespeare's *Taming of the shrew*, I.i.254, 'My lord you nod, and do not mind the play' (1596). It survives in modern form in 'mind your own business' and 'mind the gap'.

ministry Service to people, usually spoken.

motion An inward prompting or impulse; an instigation from within; e.g. Bacon in 1607, 'There is in man's nature a secret inclination, a motion, towards love of others'[32]. More specifically, 'a working of God in the soul' (OED), e.g. the collect in The Book of Common Prayer of 1548, 'That we may ever obey thy godly motions'.

naked Exposed to view; figuratively, without the cover of show or pretence. Cf. Hebrews 4:12f: 'The word of God is quick, and powerful... and is a discerner of the thoughts and intents of the heart. Neither is there any creature that is not manifest in his sight: but all things are naked and opened unto the eyes of him with whom they have to do.'

nature (1) The creative and controlling force in the material world, as in much modern use, (2) the character of a person, as in R. Steele in 1709: 'Men may change their climate, but they cannot their nature'[33]. **In this second sense** 'nature' can sometimes be described as a being in its own right; e.g. in W. Temple in 1668: 'There are some natures in the world who never can proceed sincerely in business'[34]. Fox seems to like this turn of phrase, e.g. in 2:68.

notion (1) Idea, concept; as in Thomas Browne in 1643, 'Charity, without which faith is a mere notion, and of no existence'[35]; (2) theory, belief, opinion; e.g. C. Leslie in 1697, 'It will be very hard... to make sense of the Quaker notion of the light within'[36], which is ironical indeed!

occasion (1) A reason or ground for an action: 'If ever people... had occasion to praise God, we are they'[37]; (2) what brings an event or situation about, a cause: 'Heresies... which may be an occasion of sedition'[38], and Fox's 'occasion of all wars' (3:42,43); (3) opportunity.

open Reveal, open up. Cf. Luke 24:31f,45, concerning the disciples' meeting with Jesus: 'Their eyes were opened, and they knew him; and he vanished out of their sight. And they said one to another, Did not our heart burn within us, while he talked with us by the way, and while he opened to us the scriptures?... Then opened he their understanding, that they might understand the scriptures'.

original It can mean not only the first, but the originator of all the rest, as in Coverdale's translation of the Bible in 1535 (*Ecclesiasticus*.10:13), 'Pride is the original of all sin', which may lie behind Fox's description of the devil in 1:48.

out Fox has a strong use of this word; when he says the devil is 'out of the truth' (3:72) he means he has deliberately gone out of it, i.e. abandoned it (cf. 1:45-52). Similarly, being 'in the truth' is being consciously committed to it.

outward External, as in Shakespeare's *Measure for measure*, III.ii.286, 'Oh, what may man within him hide, though angel on the outward side?'. So 'the outward' is the outside or 'the externals', as in Shakespeare's *Cymbeline*, I.i.23, 'So fair an outward, and such stuff within'. Cf. 'inward' above.

over Above, usually, implying freedom from whatever is below, or power over it (as in 3:55, where 'above' is also used). Cf. our modern sense when we say e.g. 'the manager is over her team'. Contrast 'into' above, as in 3:56.

particulars A particular is an individual person. 'In one's own particular' is in one's own case. E.g. W. Rand in 1657, 'This loss... concerns the whole Commonwealth, as much as mine own particular'[39]. But in the plural it refers to a personal matter as distinct from a public or general one – see, for example, E. Nicholas in 1653, 'Going to England in about a fortnight upon some particulars of his own'[40]. So, for someone to 'come to the truth in their own particulars' (1:34) is to discover the truth in their own individual lives, or through their own personal experience.

plunge It can mean 'immerse', as it does today, but it can also mean 'overwhelm with difficulty' or 'embarrass', as in 2:44. Cf. the *Religio. clerici* of 1681: 'I am more and more plunged and puzzled in this point'[41].

power 'The power' is shorthand for the power of the Spirit in a person or a group to live according to the light, that is, the power to resist the tendencies to live deceitfully and selfishly. The power could be felt physically, in quaking, and it could also affect other people, e.g. to convince them of the truth or to heal them. In general, Fox seems to use the word when people are deeply moved or affected by what happens.

premunire Or 'praemunire' was a writ, charging a person with refusing to accept the authority of the sovereign, on the assumption that it implied loyalty to someone else, such as the pope. To 'be premunired' is to be served a writ with this charge, often leading to imprisonment or distraint of goods. Cf. J. Day, in 1608: 'I have wronged the prince, I stand in compass of a praemunire'[42].

principle 'Fundamental source from which something proceeds; the ultimate basis upon which the existence of something depends' (OED). Cf. the philosopher John Smith in 1673: 'The scripture speaks of Christ not only as a particular person, but as a divine principle in holy souls'[43].

prize To value highly, as in J. Flavel in 1681, 'When we would express the value of a thing, we say we prize it as our eyes'[44].

professor Not an academic, but someone who professes faith, often contrasted with someone who genuinely 'possesses' it.

prove To test, try out, demonstrate, verify.

pure 'The pure in you' is 'that of God in you' which is free from moral confusion and temptation and 'which purifies you' morally. Cf. Matthew 5:8: 'Blessed are the pure in heart; for they shall see God'.

Ranters   A religious group of the time which abandoned any notion of a moral law and followed their own impulses; sometimes confused with Quakers! Hence the Quakers' 'gospel order' (see above).

reach   'To succeed in touching… to succeed in affecting or influencing by some means; to convince, win over' (OED). Cf. the Quaker Thomas Ellwood in 1713, 'Being sensible that I was thoroughly reached; and the work of God rightly begun in me'[45], and W. Dixon on the Quaker William Penn in 1851, 'Men's opinions must be reached by reason, not by force'[46].

reprobate   Someone rejected by God; someone who has fallen away from grace or religion. Cf. 2 Corinthians 13:5, from where Fox probably takes the word: 'Know ye not your own selves, how that Jesus Christ is in you, except ye be reprobates?'.

rudiments   A compression of 'rude elements', basic principles. For 1:41 see Colossians 2:8,20.

run in/into   To get involved in, incur; e.g. Shakespeare in 1613, 'I am sorry that the Duke of Buckingham is run in your displeasure' (*Henry VIII*, I.ii.110); and King James II in 1692, 'I… would have you avoid those faults I have run into'[47]. Cf. 'into' above, and contrast 'over'.

salvation   The saving of the soul (from inner conflict, loss or destruction); more specifically, the liberation of the soul from 'sin' (see below). In Puritan theology this meant primarily freedom from the condemnation and punishment that sin brought with it. For Fox it was more experiential: it was freedom from 'the power of sin', i.e. the powerful inclination to act against one's conscience.

seed   There are two quite different meanings, that are often fused in Fox: (1) the human seed as offspring or descendant, which can be applied to Christ as 'the seed of Abraham' or of Eve, or to the people of God who receive the promises made to Eve's and Abraham's seed: cf. Genesis 3:15, where God says to the serpent about Eve, 'I will put enmity between thee and the woman, and between thy seed and her seed; it shall bruise thy head, and thou shalt bruise his heel', which Fox read as a promise of victory over evil; and Galatians 3:8,16: 'The scripture, foreseeing that God would justify the heathen through faith, preached before the gospel unto Abraham, saying, In thee shall all the nations be blessed.... Now to Abraham and his seed were the promises made. He saith not, And to seeds, as of many; but as of one, And to thy seed, which is Christ' (see under 'covenant' above); (2) The seed of a plant in the ground, understood as an image of the potential for life in human beings. In this sense the seed is in people, even if buried and unrecognised; in the first sense people are in the seed, when they consciously receive the promises made. But Christ is the seed in both senses, which allows Fox to fuse the two.

settle (1) To establish or set up (an institution or business, etc.) in a particular town or country, as Fox 'settled a meeting'; cf. A. Lovell in 1687, 'This might be made one of the richest cities in the world, because of the commerce that might be settled there'[48]; and William Penn in 1694, 'Being the first monthly meeting that was settled for Friesland'[49]; (2) to ensure the stability or permanence of something; cf. the philosopher John Locke in 1693, 'Thus much for the settling your authority over your children in general'[50]; (3) to come to rest after flight or wandering, which is close to our modern sense of 'settling down'. Both the second and third meanings seem to be present in 2:36 when Fox suggests, first, that ministry that comes from God 'settles others in the life' and, second, that 'the work now is to settle and stay in the life', that is, to 'settle down' in the life and not go wandering off for nourishment elsewhere. Cf. 'gad'.

sin An act considered as an offence against God, or against the conscience; a violation of religious or moral principle.

single 'Simple, honest, sincere, single-minded; free from duplicity or deceit' (OED). E.g. Shakespeare in 1613, 'I speak it with a single heart, my Lords' (Henry VIII, V.iii.38); and J. Ford in 1633, 'Sure, he's an honest, very honest gentleman; a man of single meaning'[51].

spirit From the Latin *spiritus*, 'breath, air', it is the animating principle when applied to humans, or the immaterial centre as opposed to the material body. The 'spirit of God' is the power in God to inspire and energise human beings. To distinguish it from the human spirit or an 'evil spirit' it is sometimes also called the 'holy spirit' or 'holy ghost'.

stay upon (1) To wait on, attend to; as in Shakespeare's *Measure for measure*, IV.i.47: 'I have a servant comes with me along that stays upon me'; (2) (of the eye or mind) to dwell on, rest on, fix on; as in Isaiah 26:3, 'Thou wilt keep him in perfect peace, whose mind is stayed on thee'.

steeple house A building with a steeple, i.e. a 'church' as most people understood that word, but 'church' was a word which, in Fox's view, should not be applied to a building (cf. 2:10). 'Steeple house' had been used as an alternative before, e.g. by F. Quarles in 1644, 'When steeplehouses or meeting-places were built, which papists call churches'[52]. Cf. 'mass house' above.

tender (1) Adj: sensitive, like a plant or a wound, but applicable to human beings; 'susceptible to moral or spiritual influence; impressionable, sympathetic' (OED). Cf. our own 'tender conscience'. (2) Verb: to make an offer, but sometimes, to offer to do something (rare, but applicable to 2:82).

testimony A solemn witness or confession in public, a protest, either by word or action; cf. Milton in 1667, 'Thou... for the testimony of truth hast borne universal reproach'[53].

that of God This is an abbreviation, devised by Fox himself it seems, of a phrase such as 'that of God in thee which purifies' or 'that in thee which shows thee thyself'. 'The relative clause may also be altogether omitted so that "that of God", in this or some slightly different form, becomes a short way of referring to the Light Within' (Seppänen, 183). Sometimes, when he wishes to make a point very clear, which is not so often (!), he will use the phrase 'something of God' or 'something in thee': e.g. 'There is something of the invisible power of God in every man and woman' (3:15), and 'There is something in them that tells them that they should not practise those evils'.

time Apart from the normal meanings (as in 1:1, 1:12, 'now you have time prize it'), it can also have a more metaphysical meaning, contrasting it with eternity. Time is then all that is limited, finite, changeable. To 'comprehend time' (3:10) is to understand the temporal nature of everything, the transience and uncertainty of life. It is very similar to what Fox has in mind in 3:13: 'ye will comprehend all that which is to change, with that which doth not change and hath no end'.

tithes A tithe was a tenth part of the annual produce of a farm, a smallholding or whatever, which had to be paid, often in kind, for the support of the priesthood.

truth Truth could have three general meanings: (1) reality itself, in distinction from any imitation, representation or misrepresentation; e.g. the Quakerly Elizabeth Browning in 1844, 'The golden-hearted daisies witnessed... to the truth of things... and I woke to nature's real'[54]; (2) an agreement with reality, in a statement, an image, or some other form; e.g. J. Young in 1829, 'Truth is the agreement of our ideas and words with the nature of things'[55]; and, when applied to a human life (3) living according to reality, as in G. Burnet in 1680, 'Truth is a rational creature's acting in conformity to itself in all things'[56], which is what we might now call integrity, or truthfulness. In Fox the first sense is primary: truth is the reality beyond our 'deceit' and selfish distortion. Ultimately it is the reality of God. In the second sense, Friends could be urged to 'speak truth' and even 'preach truth', although the truth was never identified with what could be said, since words by themselves ('without the life') were a 'vain invented form' (2:39; cf. 2:67,68); 'truth is reached... beyond words' (1:44). In the third sense, Friends could 'dwell in the truth' (2:59), 'live' in it (1:41), 'practise it' (3:48), which meant truth had a moral and practical quality. Indeed, it was by accepting truth about oneself and acting on it that the larger 'truth of God' became accessible (1:33,34). So the difference between the three senses of truth begins to disappear. 'The senses which seem to stem from different sources are merged and "Truth" in all of its occurrences is not an abstract notion of some form of belief, but has a strong moral connotation of a practical nature' (Seppänen, 125). It is therefore surprising, and alarming, that the OED adds as an example of 'the truth, denoting a particular form of belief', 'esp. in Quaker language; 1662 *Extr. S. P. Rel. Friends* II, 144, "It is ordered that there be a collection this month for the service of the truth"; 1710, O. Sansom, *Acc Life*, 40, "The Friend was declaring the truth, when the priest... came in"'. See Essay.

try   To test.

walk   Figuratively, to live in a certain way, to behave (well or badly); e.g. J. Flavel in 1681, 'When a man walks suitably to his place and calling in the world, we say he acts like himself'[57].

want   To want is to lack, to miss; *a* want is a need.

will-worship   Worship devised by the human will, rather than God's.

withal   'Which... withal' = 'with which' or 'with whom'. When Fox says 'this is the light which you are lighted withal' (1:69) he means 'this is the light with which you are enlightened'. Compare 3:28 and 3:31.

without   Outside, the opposite of 'within'; figuratively, outside the inward being, the heart or mind; sometimes, in outward appearance as opposed to inward reality. Cf. 'outward' above.

witness To witness is not to see, as it is today, but to bear witness to what one has seen. So 'to witness to the truth' is 'to bear witness to what one has seen of the truth'. This can be applied to the light within, which is 'the witness of God' in people, and to the words and actions of people who have already embraced the truth and live by it.

world Society outside the community of Friends, often with the implication that it is devoted to 'worldly', i.e. secular interests. This negative reading was taken largely from John's Gospel (e.g. John 1:10; 8:12; 12:47; 14:27).

wrought Done, in the sense of performed; e.g. P. Francis in 1746, 'Let not such upon the stage be brought, which better should behind the scenes be wrought'[58]. When Fox says 'your works will be wrought in God' (1:87) he means 'your actions will be performed in God', or 'what you do will be done in God'.

ENDNOTES for glossary

1. John Daus, trans. (1561) Bullinger's Hundred sermons upon the Apocalypse, 144b.
2. John Milton (1667) Paradise lost, 10.862.
3. Thomas Holcroft, trans. (1793) Lavater's Essays on physiognomy, 131, 163.
4. William Penn (1694) The rise and progress of the people called Quakers, 2.45.
5. William Fenner (1657) Christ's alarm, 25.
6. Edward Gibbon (1781) The history of the decline and fall of the Roman empire, 28.5.3.80.
7. John Milton (1667) Paradise lost, 11.212.
8. William Blackstone (1765-9), Commentaries on the laws of England, 2.484.
9. John Donne (1628) Sermons, on 1 Corinthians 13:12.
10. John Milton (1667) Paradise lost, 3.195.
11. Joseph Butler (1725) Fifteen sermons, 2.
12. Westminster Assembly of Divines (1647) Shorter catechism, A.12.
13. Westminster Assembly of Divines (1647) Westminster larger catechism, A.31.
14. R. Brooke (1641) English episcopacy, 2.7.121.
15. William Tyndale (1531) Exposition of the epistles of St. John, on 1 John 1:5.
16. E. Walker (1692) Epicteti enchiridion, 'to the author'.
17. George Chapman (1615) The whole works of Homer in his Iliads and Odysseus, vii.290.

18. John Preston (1628) The new covenant, 2.32.

19. R. Harvey (1593) Philadelphus, 10.6.

20. Joseph Hall (1644) Sermons, 110.

21. W. de W. (1526) The pilgrimage of perfection, 9.

22. T. Boston (1732) The crook in the lot, 15.

23. John Milton (1641) Of prelatical episcopacy, 6.

24. Gilbert Burnet (1688) Letters of the state of Italy, 11.

25. Robert Barclay (1676) The apology, prop. 5 & 6.§23.

26. John Davies, trans. (1662) Olearius' Voyages and travels of the ambassadors, 67.

27. John Milton, Works, 144.

28. Thomas Cogan (1584) The haven of health, 212, 216.

29. Francis Rous, Treatises and meditations, 230f.

30. W. Allen (1674) Danger of enthusiasm, 105.

31. John Pearson (1659) Exposition of the Creed.

32. Francis Bacon (1607) Essays, 'On love', 449.

33. Richard Steele (1709) The Tatler, no. 93, p. 4.

34. William Temple (1668) Works, 2.119.

35. Thomas Browne (1643) Religio medici, 11.§1.

36. Charles Leslie (1697) The snake in the grass, 12.

37. Robert Hill (1610) The pathway to prayer and piety, preface.

38. John Daus, trans. (1560) Sleidanes Commentaries, 4b.

39. W. Rand, trans. (1657) Gassendi's Mirror of true nobility, 2.281.

40. E. Nicholas (1653) The Nicholas papers, 2.22.

41. Religio clerici (1681), 188.

42. John Day (1608) Law-Trickes, 75.

43. John Smith (1673) Discourses, 451.

44. John Flavel (1681) The method of grace, 35.583.

45. Thomas Ellwood (1713) The history of the life of Thomas Ellwood, 45.

46. William Dixon (1851) William Penn, an historical biography, 10.83.

47. James II (1692) in T. Longueville, Adversus James II, 28.478.

48. A. Lovell (1687) *Thevenot's travels into the Levant*, 2.157.

49. William Penn (1694) *William Penn's travels in Holland and Germany*, 162.

50. John Locke (1693) *Some thoughts concerning education*, 4.1.43.

51. John Ford (1633) *The broken heart*, 4.1.

52. Francis Quarles (1644) *Whipper whipt*, in *Works*, 1.161-2.

53. John Milton (1667) *Paradise lost*, 6.33.

54. Elizabeth Browning (1844) 'The lost bower', *Poetical works*, 47.

55. J. Young (1829) *Lectures on intelligence and philosophy*, 38.382.

56. Gilbert Burnet (1680) *The life and death of John earl of Rochester*, 55.

57. John Flavel (1681) *The method of grace*, 30.323.

58. P. Francis (1746) *Horace: art and poetry*, 264.

ESSAY

making sense of Fox

MAKING SENSE OF FOX

1

Fox was an unusual kind of teacher. He travelled over the country to teach people not to rely on human teachers. We can see this paradox in the first extract of the Anthology (1:1). It comes from an early letter in which he reminds the people of Ulverston why he had come to speak to them. We have too few accounts of his initial preaching, and this is a particularly clear one, articulated at the point when the mission was about to take off. 'I was moved of the Lord to come into your public places to speak among you, being sent of God to direct your minds to him, that you might know where to find your teacher.' This would have been as surprising to the people of Ulverston as it is to us. They would have expected a travelling preacher to preach his doctrine. That, after all, is what the Puritans had been doing for many years now, and even the more radical preachers such as the Baptists and the Independents who told people to rely on the spirit taught them nonetheless the doctrines they needed to know. But Fox refused to do that. He had no doctrines, as they would have understood that word. Instead, he urged them to look inside them for a teacher. 'Your teacher is within you', he concludes, 'look not forth'. The people of Ulverston were not pleased, least of all William Lampitt, the Puritan minister of the town, who would have concluded, rightly, that this message could undermine his whole ministry and therefore his livelihood.

In any case, the Puritan teaching was quite clear: only those who were educated in the study of the scriptures could be fit to teach the common people. Otherwise every Tom, Dick and Harry will think they are entitled to preach 'as they are led by the spirit'. Fox's letter must have confirmed that fear, because he goes out of his way to assure the common people that even the worst of them, the 'liars, drunkards, whoremongers and thieves', have a measure of the spirit in them which is sufficient at least to steer them away from those evils they despise.

Fox evidently saw it as his mission to awaken that spirit in people and to encourage them to trust it. This was also his advice to those who felt similarly called to spread the truth they had discovered for themselves: 'If you would have them come to the knowledge of truth, let them know it, and where it is to be found' (3:24). Surprising as it may be, the advice is not to tell them what the truth is!

But Fox never thought that this would be an easy or straightforward matter. Not only did people lack the confidence to trust a source of truth within them, but they were also afraid of what it might reveal. Why should they 'love the light' (1:1) when it was supposed to show them 'sin, evil and deceit'? They would much rather have a doctrine that reassured them about their state. 'Yet you in your darkness', i.e. lack of awareness, 'will go make an image of God, of the bigness of a corruptible man.... You make images of God like yourselves' (1:4). Religions are generally invented by human beings to make them feel better about their situation or to help them to accept their situation in the hope of something better after death (1:5). Far from leading people into truth they give them illusions and comfortable pictures.

It could be said that images and pictures are meant to point beyond themselves to the reality they represent. But this was not Fox's experience. He found they got in the way, not because they misrepresented reality but because they expressed it in a concrete, 'outward form', and therefore drew people's attention away from their inner reality to this external object, whatever it was. People then trust the object – the liturgy, the sermon, the Bible – and put their hopes in that. But they may soon be disillusioned (1:10; cf. 3:47), as Fox was himself. And it was only when he himself was thoroughly disillusioned with all external objects, and especially other human beings, that he discovered the truth within: 'then, O then I heard a voice' (1:13). The difference was that he was now experiencing the reality for himself, directly, not having to depend on an uncertain intermediary. 'This I knew experimentally'.

When we look at this closely it becomes clear that Fox was doing for religion what Galileo and Newton were doing for science. He was rejecting knowledge that was passed on by authorities and he was testing the matter for himself by looking to experience. The new scientists brought about a revolution in science by looking at physical phenomena for themselves and deriving what knowledge they could from that. The result might seem paltry compared with the grand systems of Aristotle and Ptolemy, but it was sound and firm and its truth could be made evident to anyone. It could also be built on, and anyone seriously interested could make a contribution. Blind faith was no longer required. This new outlook affected many other spheres of life, such as art and politics. But not religion, which stuck firmly to authority and tradition as the source of its truth and so steadily became alienated from the wider culture – except in the case of Fox and the early Friends. They took the risk, as William Penn put it, of undertaking an 'experiment upon the soul',[1] so that others should 'not believe upon my authority, nothing less – for that's not to act upon knowledge, but trust – but that thou shouldst try and approve what I write, for that is all I ask.... It is self-evident to them that will uprightly try it'.[2] Notice the experimental tenor of 1:21: 'So the power of the mighty God know (the arm), and how it works, and the hand how it carries you, which brings out of tribulation... into peace'.

Not that it was there simply for the looking. 'The pearl... is hid'

(1:23), and everyone should therefore 'be digging for the pearl' in their own field (1:17). As becomes clear later in the Anthology, the treasure is buried in the earth, covered by deceit and the pre-occupation with outward things. 'When your minds run into anything outwardly, without the power, it covers and veils the pure in you' (1:54). But why should people be so taken with outward things that they are unable to see the truth within them? Fox's answer is strikingly original, anticipating insights that were not to emerge fully for hundreds of years. They are preoccupied with outward things precisely because they cannot face the truth inside them, especially the truth about themselves. It so contradicts the image they have of themselves, or want to have of themselves, that they deny the truth, they turn a blind eye to it (1:55). So the truth they dimly perceive, but won't accept, is put on to other things or other people. For example, when they read about evil people in the Bible they 'do not see the nature of Cain, of Esau, of Judas and those others, in themselves. These said it was they, they, they that were the bad people, *putting it off from themselves*' (1:27, my emphasis). In our language we would say they *projected* it on to others. Having done that they can then feel much better about themselves, seeing themselves as 'righteous', and they can feel con-fident that the picture of God and themselves they have secretly imagined is really the truth.

All this amounts to 'deceit', which Fox evidently saw as the main blight on human beings. For once they deny the truth about them-selves they 'are given over to believe lies' (1:45), and once that happens they are lost, for they can see nothing as it really is. They live 'in darkness'. And this in turn is the source of all their misery: 'for all the sufferings', he says in a rather Buddhist line of thought, 'are by and through him that is out of the truth' (1:49). The 'him' in this case is the devil, and it is striking that Fox speaks of the devil whenever he ponders the reason for this blight on human beings. I take this to mean that he finds the reason mysterious and has to resort to mythological language to speak of it. Why, after all, should people choose to live in darkness when they could live in the light? Why should they prefer a make-believe world to the world of reality? Why should they put all their hopes on tangible objects and human constructions which, as we shall see, inevitably let people down (e.g. 3:47)?

Is this a despairing vision of humanity? Not really. The power of darkness or the devil lies in their ability to 'seduce' human beings (1:29) from their own immediate awareness of reality into believing something that will be apparently more satisfactory. If it turns out **not** to be satisfactory, however, humans can always reject it and return to the truth which they already in some sense know. All they have to do is 'turn' from one to the other; no great education is required, not even a great spiritual journey. They are already close to the light, but pointed away from it, pretending it isn't there. They have only to turn on the spot and they will see the truth they need to know (1:57,59).

This says something about the kind of truth they need to know, though for us, some three hundred years later, this may not be so easy to grasp. We are used to thinking of truth in quite objective terms, as in 'scientific truth' or truth in opposition to error or misrepresentation. We see it, in other words, as a quality of words: truth is a correct statement, a correct set of ideas. So if anyone makes bold to talk about the truth, especially if they want to claim it is the truth, we expect them to spell it out in words so that we can judge for ourselves. Nowadays, of course, we are more likely to be sceptical about such claims, not because we have a better account to offer, but because we seriously question whether any such account is possible. We are so aware of how many belief systems there are, and how readily they change over time and differ from place to place, that they seem like all too human attempts to grasp the ungraspable. The philosophers among us may say that our language is simply not designed to grasp reality as a whole, since it is always only human language, and humans are limited, time-bound creatures who speak from and to their own limited situation. With all this (possibly) in our minds we are not likely to be impressed when we hear Fox telling people to 'come to the truth' and base their lives on it.

Whether we are moderns who expect truth to be articulated in a coherent set of ideas, or postmoderns who think any such attempt is futile, we will agree at least that truth belongs to words. So it is natural for us, as it was indeed for the Puritans of his own day, to expect Fox, if he must speak about the truth, to state what he believed the truth to be so that we in turn can consider whether to believe it. And that in fact is how Fox has mostly been understood, even by those who take him most seriously. A recent 'glossary' of Fox's language defined 'truth' as a summary of the Quaker message.

But if we read Fox this way we will soon find it difficult to make sense of him, and may well conclude that it is Fox himself who is confused, as has often been said. A typical example of his 'confusion' would be an injunction such as the following: 'Take heed of knowledge, for it puffeth up, but dwell in the truth, and be what ye speak' (2:73). How can you 'dwell in the truth' and at the same time disregard 'knowledge'? Perhaps he was thinking of the vaunted knowledge of the dons of Oxford and Cambridge, and proffering his own 'truth' as an alternative, in which case we might have to dismiss him as a bigot and an obscurantist! But consider another text in which he seems to be getting into the same confusion: 'Take heed of words without life, for they tend to draw you out of the power to live above the truth, and out of your conditions; which nature will not have peace, except it have words' (2:68). Again, we are being asked to make a choice between 'words' and 'the truth', as if the two could be separated! But perhaps Fox seriously thought they could be and should be separated. Perhaps he meant something else by 'truth' than what could be formulated in words. This is the suspicion raised by these texts.

Notice how living 'above the truth' is equated with being 'out of your conditions', which means cut off from the reality of your own experience, your actual situation. 'Words without life' are conjuring up a fanciful idea about your life, which prevents you from seeing what is really happening in your life. Now that makes sense. So too with the first quotation: we can see on reflection that 'dwell in the truth' is to be equated with, or brought very close to, 'be what ye speak', which is an appeal for integrity. 'Dwell in the truth' is not now so odd as a piece of advice if it means 'live your life on the basis of reality', or, as we might say, 'be real'. In fact it makes a lot of sense, though it does now sound like quite strong advice!

The suspicion raised by these examples is that for Fox 'truth' does not mean in the first place a representation of reality, whether in words or images, but reality itself. The suspicion is confirmed when we discover that the word 'reality' hardly existed in the seventeenth century and only then among the educated few, and that what we understand by the term was covered then by the word 'truth'. So truth then was a richer, broader concept than it is now. It was possible then to say that philosophers sought truth in their reasoning *and* that an honest man sought truth in being faithful to his wife *and* that a religious person sought truth by praying. In all their different ways they were trying to be true to what is, looking for or holding on to reality.

So when Fox came declaring that people should find the truth in themselves and live in truth and practise it in all their affairs, they all knew what he meant, though the Puritans among them would have frowned at his untutored talk. In fact, his use of common language in tackling the big issues of their lives would have made Fox especially appealing to the common people. So with this broad understanding of the word, truth was not to be 'believed', any more than reality is to be believed. It was to be faced and accepted, and 'lived in', made the basis of one's life. Truth was the reality of one's life which is always there to be experienced if only one is open to it. The only trouble is that people won't or can't face the truth and so opt for a make-believe world instead, which they then become so attached to that they are no longer aware of the reality they are denying.

That is why Fox says that 'everyone is… to come to the truth in their own particulars', i.e. in their own personal experience, and 'in their own hearts' (1:34). This is not to say that the truth they need to know is only about them, but that it has to start with them, because until they face the reality they are turning a blind eye to (1:55) they won't be able to see anything else. 'If all men would come to the knowledge of the truth they must come to that which doth reprove them, and lead them into all truth' (1:72). That tells us both why people are so reluctant to face the truth and yet also, at the same time, how simple it would be to find it.

But how are they to find it? Hasn't Fox now talked himself into a corner, saying on the one hand that people must find the truth in themselves, and on the other hand that they are no longer able or willing to do so? This was indeed a dilemma for Fox and for the whole movement he helped to get going. He had two responses to this dilemma, both of which were essentially practical. That is, his response was not to try to explain the situation, in a doctrine of grace and free will for example, but to tell people what to do so that they could experience the situation for themselves and come to a realisation of 'the truth in their own particulars'. A surprising amount of his writing, in fact, is taken up with giving advice: suggesting what people should do rather than what they should think. But his first advice was always the same: 'Mind the pure light of God in you' (1:83), 'Mind your measure' (1:1), 'Let the light of Jesus Christ, that shines in every one of your consciences, search you thoroughly, and it will let you clearly see' (1:82). So they were initially to pay attention to something that was already quite apparent, their conscience. This would tell them what was right and wrong in their lives, or at least give them a feeling of unease about something. They were then to pay attention to that something and let the light in their conscience show them what was really going on there (1:75,78,83,87). If they were sufficiently open to what the light had to show them it would show them everything, the whole reality of their lives.

But this second step was not so easy, because although they could recognise twinges of conscience, 'there has so much strife and foolishness entered the minds of people, and a want of stillness and quietness in the pure spirit of God, in which things are revealed that have been veiled' (1:67), that they gain no insight into themselves. They need to learn to be quiet, to be 'still and cool' in their minds (1:61). The activities of 'the self' have to be slowed right down, at least temporarily, so that something else can be brought into play. The 'light of God' is certainly within people, but it is not part of their normal mental make-up. It is not part of the ego, or the conscious personality – that 'you must die in the silence' (1:63)! And only when they are 'still and cool... from their own thoughts' will they 'then... feel the principle of God to turn [their] mind to the Lord God' (1:61). But what people are being urged to do here is really to stop doing anything! They have simply to pay attention to what is happening, without intervening in the situation with their own thoughts, plans, arguments or imaginings, and then they will experience something else happening that is not of their own doing. They will find, for example, that whereas before they had been confused about their lives they are now able to see them clearly (1:82), that they can now understand what makes them tick (1:83) and, above all, that it is the self, always, that gets in the way of seeing things clearly (1:84,85) and makes them do the things they ultimately despise (1:87). All this may be very painful, but it will at least be recognised as the truth about themselves.

So Fox's first response to the dilemma is to tell people, in effect, that the truth *is accessible*, because whatever their attitude or confusion or sense of inadequacy there is always the twinge of conscience that can lead them to the truth. It is like Ariadne's thread: Ariadne was concerned that if Theseus entered the labyrinth he would never be able to find his way out, so she gave him a ball of thread to unroll on the ground as he made his way in.

His second response to the dilemma is to say that however worrying the truth may be when it is first encountered, *truth liberates* (1:40,41,121; 2:94; 3:84). People are not to take their first experience of the truth, let alone their ideas of what it might be, as the last word on the subject. For the process that begins in 'minding the light' continues: in simply attending to the light, quite passively, they find that the reality of their lives is disclosed to them. If they then stay with that reality and don't avert their eyes, still more will be disclosed (1:88,89).

The discomfort of self-disclosure will of course make people want to turn away, and perhaps return to their comfortable illusions. But Fox urges them to 'stand, neither go to the right hand nor to the left; here patience is exercised' (1:89), because what happens next, provided they 'submit' to the truth being revealed, i.e. accept it, is that they begin to experience a reversal of what had made them miserable. They experience 'mercy' for what they have done wrong, then contentment and peace, because the struggle to maintain the self-deception is over, and finally 'power and strength' to overcome the desires that had led them to act wrongly or unwisely in the first place (1:89-91).

In fact, if they stay with the light and all it has to show them, they will experience everything they had heard of the gospel from the pulpit or witnessed in the liturgy, but they will experience it for themselves, directly, without the mediation of any external form or notion. They will 'see God' (1:92,93), not through a stained-glass window, but 'with the spiritual eye' and from a pure heart (1:94). They will hear Christ, the true mediator between God and humans (1:100), speaking in their own hearts (1:99,101), and hearing him and responding to him they will find themselves reconciled to God, though they had long been alienated from God (2:18). And having in this way discovered their true nature, their true relationship to God, they will come to life (1:120-123). The old self dies (1:63,89) because it is false, an image constructed to stave off harsh reality, but unable to sustain itself when exposed to the light: 'now all loving the light here no self can stand… and no self-will can arise, no mastery' (1:84). And a new self is born (1:122,123), 'the hidden man in the heart' (2:14) that was concealed and repressed by the pretentious ego, like a seed held down by the hard winter soil (1:105,106), but is now liberated by the light, like the seed in springtime (1:107).

This is the promise Fox holds out for those about to venture on the path and undergo the rigours of exposing themselves to truth. He is bearing witness to his own experience of where the path of truth leads. He claims no special divine authority for what he says, as if they were simply to accept his word for it. He says, certainly, that he is sent by God to speak to them, but what he has to tell them is how they can discover truth for themselves: the truth itself will do the rest, or, what comes to the same thing, the light within them will do the rest because it will show them the truth (cf.1:1). They do not have to believe anything in fact, not even what they were told from the pulpit, because they will discover all they need to know by opening up their hearts to the reality immediately in front of them. Then, having discovered that there *is* a capacity within them to see themselves as they are (cf.1:129), and that this knowledge of themselves is liberating and powerful and life-giving (1:120,121), they will want to speak of 'the light of God' inside them. They will experience things so far beyond their normal human capacities that they will have to resort to the language of transcendence to speak about them, to use words again such as spirit, Christ and the infinite God.

2

All this is addressed to the individual, to begin with, and necessarily, because each individual has to discover the truth of their own situation before they can experience it more widely. 'Every man, every woman', he says emphatically, 'must come to the spirit of God in their own selves' (1:30; cf.1:34; 2:14), so as to experience reality directly without the mediation of ideas, images or even other people. In emphasising this and in helping to establish this as a viable practice Fox was pushing religion further than it had ever gone before towards the responsibility of the individual.[3] But this was not to deny the importance of the group or the community. On the contrary, he urged individual friends to recognise their need of one another. The individual, after all, has only a 'measure' of light, according to their 'capacity' (1:1; 2:30,90), even though it can be increased. And individuals will have a variety of gifts, according to 'the manifold grace of God' (2:30,32). So although the light within them may be fully adequate, their capacity to receive it and deploy it may not be. Friends therefore can complement one another; they can 'refresh' one another (2:7,12,13). This had to be a fairly close, mutual relationship, because they were going to have to share quite intimate truths about themselves (2:74; 3:27). So when Fox had spoken in public, often to large crowds, those who were 'convinced' by the spirit would gather in more intimate surroundings to share the experience together. Barbour and Frost describe those first meetings like this:

> Early Quaker prophetic messages of judgment and confrontation were often given in a marketplace or during a puritan church service. For longer presentations crowds of noisy but interested hearers were gathered on a moor or daily in a rented hall in an 'appointed' or 'threshing' meeting. Hearers who were 'convinced' by these forms of mission were taken into smaller gatherings in private homes, where they shared their struggles

of self-judgment under the Light with other seekers in daily or weekly 'gathered meetings' with prayer and messages of guidance as well as silence and tears.[4]

Fox would then write letters, or 'epistles' in the biblical manner, to these newly formed groups of 'Friends in the Truth' to guide them on their way. One of his primary concerns was to encourage unity and peace in the group so that they were willing and able to care for one another (e.g. 2:19,20,22,94-96). This indeed is his vision of the 'true church' (2:9): a community of friends in which each depends on the spirit within them and finds unity and love in that spirit with the others.

But this hope for communal life immediately raised a problem. The variety of Friends' gifts and capacities made a rich resource for their life together, but it also inevitably led to differences between them. How were they to cope with this? Fox's emphasis on the need for every Friend of Truth to come to this truth in their own particular experience only exacerbated the difficulty. What was there to transcend their individualities that could hold them together without also crushing them?

Fox's response was remarkably simple, although it has not been fully understood by those who have tried to interpret him. 'All they that are in the light are in unity; for the light is but one' (2:18). If we take 'the light' to refer merely to individual inspiration, which is the usual way of understanding Fox, then this statement will sound dogmatic, and certainly not be logical in the way it pretends to be. Fox would then be simply asserting that the inspirations must agree. But if we understand the light in terms of the process of enlightenment we have seen him describe, that is, as a God-given capacity to see things as they are without the distortions of self, then his statement is perfectly logical. If people judge things in terms of their own selfish viewpoint, he would be saying, they are bound to see things differently and therefore disagree. But if they see things in the light, they will transcend their individual viewpoints and be able to grasp the truth of the situation, objectively, so they are bound to agree. There is only 'one light' because there is only one reality, one truth, and the function of the light, as we have noted, is to let people see reality (1:68,129).

In practice, of course, it wouldn't have been as simple as that. Friends would still have different views, different preferences and ways of thinking, so that finding unity in a group would itself have to be a process in which they struggled to overcome the limits of self. This seems to be recognised in the passage that affirmed so confidently that 'the light is but one' (2:18), for it goes on to say that this 'word' which Friends have come to hear within them is 'a word of reconciliation, that reconcileth together to God, and gathers the hearts of his together, to live in love and unity, and lets them see how they have been strangers and aliens from the life of God'. I'm not sure whether Fox is saying that they have been strangers to each other as well as to God, but the idea would fit, because their hearts need to be 'gathered' together by God, implying that they were separated before, and possibly 'alienated' from one another. But notice how the process of gathering takes place: the light simply lets them see what they were once and what they are now. As 'strangers' they had not really seen one another at all, because, no doubt, they looked at one another as they had looked at themselves, in terms of their own self-interest. So what they saw was an image, a projection, rather than the real person. But now, 'abiding inwardly in the light', which means at least having faced the reality of their own lives, 'it will let you see one another and the unity with one another' (2:18). The light itself does the work, provided Friends allow it to, and it does it by showing the unity that is already there, despite all the prejudices and fears they might have of one another. That particular point is made clearer in 1:84, which shows how unity is achieved. Each person is to allow the light to show them themselves so that the claims of the self, the ego, will be undermined – 'here no self can stand'. When they have done that they will find that 'no self-will can arise, no mastery', no attempt to dominate or control others, no desire to see one's own view prevail, no subtle manipulation even to bring about agreement or compromise. Instead they will experience unity as something given: 'here all are in unity'.

Was that enough – to allow the light to do its work in everyone and trust the process? Apparently not. In 1656 James Nayler, a leader of the Quakers on a par with Fox, rode into Bristol on the back of a donkey, while a band of admirers threw clothes in his path to welcome the new messiah! This was just the excuse parliament had been looking for and they punished Nayler severely, not least to put fear into the hearts of anyone else who thought they had God's spirit within them. In face of the persecution that followed, the Quakers showed remarkable resolve in maintaining their faith, but they recognised too that Nayler's gross misjudgment had brought the movement into disrepute and cast serious doubt over the reliability of individual guidance. If Nayler could fall, surely anyone could!

Fox's response to the crisis was to seek a way of establishing authority among Friends without falling back into 'outward forms' or assuming authority himself. That is, he had to find a way of curbing individual inspiration without denying the inspiration itself.[5] It had to be an original response, and indeed it was. He established 'gospel order'. He travelled round the country, yet again, to advise the groups who met regularly to worship that they should set up special meetings for decision-making about the issues that concerned them (2:11,25,29). When they came to a decision in complete unity of mind, and wrote a 'minute' to that effect, that decision would then be binding. Up to that time Friends had relied on the leadership of inspired individuals such as Margaret Fell to exercise discipline and pastoral care, although groups in the north of the country had already begun to meet together to deal with problems collectively. What Fox was recommending was an extension of those 'monthly meetings' to the whole of the country. So the process that started tentatively in some areas during the early 1650s grew to embrace the whole movement, so that eventually 'quarterly' and 'yearly' meetings were also established (2:12,96); and as persecution increased in the late 1660s it became increasingly important for Friends to act as a national body and indeed to exercise discipline over those who 'walked disorderly'.

I am not persuaded by those who regard this as primarily a shift from the individual to the group.[6] There is a shift, undoubtedly, but in a slightly different direction. After all, Fox was urging Friends to form groups from the very start, and expressing his concern for the unity of the group. Two of the extracts here were written before 1656, the year of the Nayler crisis. For example, 2:20, 'For here is my grief, when I hear anything amongst Friends that hinders their unity, and makes a breach' (from 1655; cf.1:84 from 1653). And when he later came to advise collective decision-making he insisted that it should always be answerable to the light in each Friend (2:29). It wasn't the group as such that was to make the decision; it was the light in the group, as voiced through individuals, and it was that that gave the decisions authority (2:50,51). So the principles for guiding the group process were the same as those for the individual, and they still involved the individual, though in a different way. There was no change in outlook here, only a change in practice, to accommodate a new situation.

But there was also, it has to be said, a shift in balance from the small group to the large group,[7] and from the immediacy of truth to the formality of the minute. Fox's 'settling of the meetings' for decision-making was certainly effective in securing unity and collective discipline, but there was a down-side too. As the historian William Braithwaite describes it, 'the natural result was not merely to co-ordinate the discernment of the community with the spiritual leadings of the individual, but to enlarge continuously, by the successive encroachments with which a system of organisation aggrandises itself, the area of conduct over which the community exerted absolute sway'.[8] This compromise must surely have caused Fox and his friends a good deal of anxiety, but it seems they had little choice in such a hostile environment.

Given the restraints of the new gospel order it is surprising how much freedom Friends still enjoyed in their communities and how much freedom Fox still urged on them. Everyone was free to speak in their meetings, 'as he is moved' (2:36), women as well as men (2:30-34), and they were free to live their lives as the spirit led them, without submitting to external authorities such as scripture (2:44-49) or ethical codes (2:51). Perhaps Fox was thinking of the new constraints when he urged Friends in 1664 to 'keep... your first love', and not to 'go forth from your rule of faith and life within' (2:51). The light that had initially shown them themselves, and the seed of life within them, would also now show them the way to go in life (2:63).

This is parallel to the advice Fox had given about doctrines, or 'notions' as he called them. He had urged people not to rely on human teachers, priests and pastors and the like, because they had their teacher within (1:1,28,29). It also follows the advice he was giving about the group: not to rely on authority figures such as bishops, or even Fox himself, but to rely on the light to bring unity and order. Now he is saying that when they face practical problems in their lives they should once again trust the light to show them what to do. 'In the light walk' (2:66), 'in the truth live' (2:61), which means they are to conduct their lives in response to the truth that the light will show them. How that is possible is made clearer in 2:64. Let me break down the advice like this:

1. In this holy seed is the treasure of wisdom and knowledge,
2. with which wisdom and knowledge you will have understanding,
3. that all your conversation (behaviour) may be ordered by it aright,

4. and all your words may be gracious

5. that so... you may be... salt of the earth

6. that... you may be instrumental to open the eyes of others.

There are six steps here, each dependent on the one before. The first step is to turn to the seed of life within, from which a new awareness will arise, a new knowledge of oneself and the world. This awareness of reality then gives 'understanding', which I take to mean a practical understanding of what is going on in one's life and the world, because that in turn leads to 3, an ability to conduct one's life rightly, and 4, to speak to people with a loving attention to their needs. This kind of behaviour and speech can profoundly affect the world, preserving it like 'salt' preserves meat, and even awakening people to an awareness of reality, which brings the process full circle (cf. 3:71).

In all this there is no need to consult a code of behaviour to know what to do, though human writings, such as scripture, can help us to see more clearly if our eyes are already open (2:44,47). And Fox himself is not really telling people how to behave, though he does call on Friends to develop those virtues that come from the spirit (e.g. 2:77). The general tone of his advice is always to consult that deep awareness that all have inside, and then to trust it and act on it. Even when he is being specific about a situation, such as buying and selling (2:62), he guides them on how to approach the situation rather than on how precisely to act. The language can then be rather strange: 'act truth, doing justly and uprightly in all your actions... let truth be the head and practise it'. What has truth got to do with it? And how can this advice help anyone through the moral maze of the marketplace? Well, we need only recall what Fox means by truth – being true to what is, faithful to reality – and we can see that he is advising people simply to bring to their various activities the sense of reality they have gained in the light and to stick to it through thick and thin: to be real with the people they deal with, treating them as the people they are and not merely as traders, to be honest and open about the value of goods and one's own interest in selling or buying them. This is 'acting truth'.

The process that leads to right action can probably best be described as discernment (2:52-55), because discernment requires insight as well as knowledge, and the knowledge it contains is grounded in experience. It can also 'grow', a point Fox emphasises (2:54,89,90), but growth happens only when people act on the insight they already have. They must 'obey the truth of what they are convinced', otherwise they will lose whatever they have gained from it (2:60). They must be 'faithful' to the little light they have and then more will be given and they themselves will grow (2:89,90). And finally, they must 'love one another and love enemies' (2:80); or rather, if they 'come to the spirit and truth in their own hearts' they will love people quite naturally, without needing to be told, because they will 'see one another and the unity with one another' (2:1; cf. 2:3). So the process of discernment is an upward spiral: insight leads to love, love leads to action, action leads to reflection, and reflection leads to more insight. This is the process that Fox put his faith in.

We need only to add that discernment too involves the whole group, and that the group itself is a resource for everyone (2:3). Others in the group will need love and care and truth-speaking, but they in turn, by their response, will be helping too. Fox's hope for the meetings is that they will show what Christianity is by caring for one another, so that they can 'all live as a family' (2:96).

3

William Penn wrote of Fox and the first Friends that they hadn't set out deliberately to change the world, as if they had some better idea, but 'God having given them a sight of themselves they saw the whole world in the same glass of truth'.[9] The image is striking. God had given them a mirror to show them the truth, and having looked in the mirror and seen themselves, they then turned the mirror slightly to see the rest of the world. They couldn't then help being concerned about the world, Penn infers, because they could see what was really going on. That captures the spirituality of Fox perfectly.

According to his Journal, Fox first 'saw himself' in the light in the year 1647, when he was 23: 'then did I see my troubles... I did discern my own thoughts, groans and sighs' (1:75). Only one year later, in 1648, 'was I come up in the spirit through the flaming sword into the paradise of God.... The creation was opened to me' (3:1). His first sight of the world was not troubling. He saw it in its pristine glory. And this experience gave him a very positive view of the world, unlike the Puritans, who generally saw it as fallen and corrupted beyond repair. Seeing creation in the light one can see that evil and destruction are not primary: fundamentally all things are 'blessed' (3:3,4). Not that corruption and evil are denied, but they are seen to be based on deceit, the denial of truth (1:47,49). The world as we now know it, alienated from its true source, 'the world' as Fox normally understood the term, is a travesty of what it was meant to be because it is constructed by humans to serve their own selfish ends. But those ends are illusory. So creation, the world as it was meant to be, can be restored, and people can be restored if they are seen in the truth and treated accordingly (3:5,6). They are 'imprisoned' by the world of deceit (3:12,14) and only need the truth to be freed from it (3:16; cf. 1:40-42).

Of course, if people are to be freed they must respond to the truth, that is, recognise the deceit that their lives have been based on (cf. 1:3) and reject it in favour of reality. But they *can* do this because beneath the layers of falsehood they have something in them which is quite uncontaminated by falsehood and able to recognise and hold on to truth. This is 'the light' by which Fox himself came to see the truth, and by which indeed he 'saw it shine through all' (1:77). His experience told him that it must be a universal possibility, and that it must have the same divine source and authority in others that it had in him. So this now was the basis for his mission: to convey that sense of truth to other people that would free them 'from the spiritual prison of death' (3:16).

But there was a problem. If 'truth' in this sense was an immediate experience of reality how could it be conveyed to others? Words were inadequate, as we have seen, to represent reality as it is experienced in the light (2:41,42,47,68-71). And people will always find reasons for rejecting words if they don't like the implications of what they hear. How can you use words then to get beneath words (cf. 1:44)? This was not such a problem for other religious teachers of his day because they were quite ready to believe that the truth could be said, and indeed that it had been quite definitively said already, in the Bible. Their main task therefore was to 'preach the word', explaining what God 'had said in scripture' and applying it to the condition of their listeners. But Fox could not take this route. He even wanted an end to 'all outward preaching' (2:37). He had to find some other form of communication. And what he did find, though superficially not so different from that of other preachers, was in fact quite original: he was not to try and convey the truth to others as something he possessed and they did not, but to evoke the truth they already had in them, and to do this by the *way* he spoke as much as by what he spoke about, and by the way he lived.

'If you would have them come to the knowledge of truth, let them know it, and *where it is to be found*' (3:24). That advice is anticlimactic, no doubt, but it is entirely in keeping with Fox's insight. As in his own case, the truth will be found only by having the courage to look for oneself *at* oneself and face the reality head-on. That at least can be said: that people look into themselves, which is how Fox described his own mission (1:1,78). He can also try to tell them what he thinks they will find, on the basis of what he himself has found. But that is not nearly enough, because to have courage to do that, people will want to be assured that truth can be had that way, that truth is good and wholesome and liberating, and not the fearful reality it appears to be. So the *way* of speaking becomes important as a way of conveying or eliciting truth that cannot be conveyed in *what* is said. The communication must not only be about the truth, it must itself be truthful, i.e. it must be open, honest, 'plain', direct, straightforward and thoroughly consistent with one's own experience and life (3:27-30). This then will, or rather *may*, evoke the divine sense of truth people have within them (3:17). It will resonate with it, 'answer it' (3:18), both by exemplifying it in oneself and by responding to it as it seeks expression in the life of the other person. So to 'answer that of God in everyone' becomes essentially what the mission entails (3:37). And here words may not even be necessary. 'Your carriage and life may preach' (3:37): a life lived in the truth will itself exemplify the truth and that will echo the truth people know in their hearts, even when they are denying it with their heads (cf. 3:20; 1:55).

So the movement that Fox helped to initiate tended to form around a distinctive way of life, which was intended, and understood, as a 'testimony' to the truth they could not adequately express in words. To be more specific, it formed around a set of testimonies, each of which responded to a different form of evil or deceit. The refusal of Friends to use violence, for example, is described as 'a certain testimony unto all the world of the truth of our hearts in this particular' (3:42), the particular in this case being the violence readily used in the society of that time for religious and political ends. It was only twelve years since the end of the civil war, and only eleven since the king himself had been beheaded. In this very year when the 'peace declaration' was made, 1660, the king's son had returned to restore the monarchy and to crush any movement that sought to undermine it again. The

Quakers were prime suspects. Their response to accusations made against them was 'to speak the plain truth of our hearts' (2:75, also from the declaration) which persuaded them they could not and should not do violence to anyone. In any case they had been liberated from the ego-based desires which made people want to resort to violence (3:42,43). And they hoped that their active refusal of violence, more than any arguments they might offer, would persuade people to 'receive' their testimony as true. This too could take place without words, although words, like the declaration, might also sometimes be useful.

Similarly with the cause of justice. Friends' testimony to the truth 'in this particular' was a lived protest against the gross inequalities and abuses of their time, for these too were based on self-deception. The needs of the poor had been heard once again in the civil war, but despite many promises they were disregarded in the Commonwealth of the 1650s and wholly rejected with the return of the king: hierarchy and privilege were once again established. So Fox denounced the self-importance of the fashionable middle-classes which had blinded them to the reality of their world: your 'ambition and pride, loftiness and haughtiness stops the ear from hearing the Lord... and stops up the eye with which you should see yourselves, and stops up your ear from hearing the poor' (3:52). It is the preoccupation with self that makes them insensitive and that leads to ill-treatment of others and social injustice. In response to all this Friends were called to do justly in all their interactions with people, for that is to treat people as they are (3:48). It is, again, a matter of living on the basis of truth, which had given them their freedom and peace of mind, but it is also a matter of bearing witness effectively to the truth that could also free others (3:54), and of helping to establish a social order based on trust instead of fear and violence (3:58,59).

This is not to say that society in general should adopt the moral principles of Friends. Without an experience and acceptance of the truth in their own lives people would be quite unable to live a life based on truth. So until they do come to that realisation they have to rely on something else, and Fox seems to accept that people will need the law, government and even state violence to bring some justice and discipline in society (3:60f; cf. 1:95),[10] and that in so far as Friends are in society they will need them too (3:60). But he is not altogether clear on this: the long passage on government (3:61, the only place in his writings where he does explain his view) seems to say that the political leaders *ought* to base their actions on truth, which, as he says elsewhere (2:24), is the only sound basis for 'true order'.

There can be no doubt, though, that Fox saw the society of his time as failing even minimal standards of justice. So he and his friends had plenty of work to do before they could stop and ask, realistically, whether the state might be inherently incapable of delivering the justice they were looking for. Their outlook on society was essentially pragmatic, because they were focused on the reality of the present. Indeed, from 1662 to 1687 their minds were preoccupied with the violence that the state was visiting on them. But their response to this persecution was not only to plead for justice by setting forth the facts (3:61,68), so that 'truth may stand over the head of the liar' (3:68), but also to turn the injustice into a form of witness. 'Your imprisonments will reach to the prisoned that the persecutor prisons in himself' (3:69), which is of course 'that of God' which he refuses to acknowledge. The way in which suffering is accepted, without retaliation or abuse, can touch the feelings of the persecutor who may have thought that the suffering was necessary. It exposes the illusion that violence is the only answer to conflict. Fox's offer of 'the other cheek' conveys 'the truth' to his opponent so powerfully that it changes his heart, and his hatred turns to love (3:71).

But what if it doesn't work? Living the truth *may* win others, but it may just as easily make them fearful and angry, because the truth would threaten the world they had so carefully constructed to make themselves safe. Fox told Friends not to be surprised if they suffer, and go on suffering: 'They that will live godly shall suffer persecution' (3:72). 'Self-religion', i.e. religion devised by the self and devoted to the self, needs to defend itself with violence, whether it is illusory or not (3:66).

Even so, the disappointment of Fox and his Friends must have been massive.[11] Those in authority had largely rejected the new movement of the spirit, which had promised to lead the world into an era of justice and peace (3:77,78). Since the opportunity had been missed the Friends of Truth could only now wait until another such opportunity came, as it surely would (3:82), and in the meantime be faithful to the truth they had received (cf. 2:89f). In one of his last papers, from 1689, he urges Friends to 'hold fast to this hope that is set before us' (3:83).

Yet despite this shift of focus, Fox's message remains what it always was. The remarkable letter that concludes the Anthology is from 1679, when Fox was 55, and it summarises perfectly, perhaps better than he had ever done before, what his vision had been all these thirty-odd years. It celebrates truth as the source of all the good things he and others had experienced, for truth exposes all the falsehoods their lives had been based on, freeing them from the narrowness of 'self' which cut them off from life, and fills them with love for the 'universal creation' to which they truly belong, and for 'the infinite and incomprehensible God' who is the source of all truth and life and peace. It is Fox's hymn to truth.

ENDNOTES to the essay

1. William Penn, 'Preface' to *Primitive Christianity revived*, reprinted in William Penn, *The peace of Europe, the fruits of solitude and other writings*, ed. Edwin B. Bronner, Everyman, 1993, p.228.
2. Ibid.
3. Cf. H. Larry Ingle, *First among Friends: George Fox and the creation of Quakerism*, OUP, 1994, pp.52f.
4. Hugh Barbour and J. William Frost, *The Quakers*, Friends United Press, Richmond, Indiana, 1994, p.39.
5. Cf. Michael J. Sheeran, *Beyond majority rule: voteless decisions in the Religious Society of Friends*, Philadelphia Yearly Meeting, 1983, part 1; William C. Braithwaite, *Spiritual guidance in Quaker experience*, Headley Brothers, 1909; Rosemary Moore, *The Light in their consciences: the early Quakers in Britain, 1646-1666*, Pennsylvania State U.P., 2000, chapters 3,10.
6. E.g. H. Larry Ingle, *First among Friends*, OUP, 1994, pp.102f, 151, 209, 258-60, which is the most authoritative biography now available.
7. Cf. Michael J. Sheeran, *Beyond majority rule*, Philadelphia Yearly Meeting, 1983, pp.10-12, 19, 41.
8. William C. Braithwaite, *Spiritual guidance in Quaker experience*, Headley Brothers, 1909, p.66.
9. William Penn, *The rise and progress of the Quakers* (1694), reprinted in Edwin B. Bronner, ed., *The peace of Europe, the fruits of solitude and other writings*, Everyman, 1993, p.286.
10. On Fox's acceptance of state violence see Peter Brock, *The Quaker peace testimony: 1660-1914*, Sessions of York, 1990, chapter 2.
11. Cf. Christopher Hill, *The experience of defeat*, Penguin Books, 1985, chapter 5 on the early Quakers specifically.

INDEX